Are You An Ice Cream Person?

There's nothing else like ice cream, right? And among the many ice cream makers of the world one name stands out—Baskin-Robbins.

The little company that Irv Robbins and Burt Baskin started back in the mid-1940s has become an American byword for quality, originality, and wholesome good taste—because Irv and Burt cared about their product. Today, nearly thirty-one years after that first batch of ice cream, love is still one of the secret ingredients in every drop of their product.

When ice cream people get together—and this is an area where "experts" of all ages abound—it's anybody's guess as to what the great new flavor favorite will be. But it's a sure thing that Baskin-Robbins made it!

If you picked up this book you're obviously an ice cream person. So are we. Here's how you can discover a whole new world of ice cream fantasy, fun, and flavor.

Imagine, an ice cream cookbook!

ICE CREAM WORLD
OF
BASKIN-ROBBINS

BY THOMAS P. JONES

PINNACLE BOOKS • NEW YORK CITY

THE ICE CREAM WORLD OF BASKIN-ROBBINS

An original Pinnacle Books edition, published for the first time anywhere.

Please note that Jamoca® is a Registered Trademark of the Baskin-Robbins Ice Cream Company.

Eight lines from "Two Tramps In Mud Time" by Robert Frost, is reprinted by permission of Holt, Rinehart and Winston, Inc. and Jonathan Cape, Ltd., from THE POETRY OF ROBERT FROST, edited by Edward Connery Lathem. Copyright 1936 by Robert Frost. Copyright © 1964 by Lesley Frost Ballantine. Copyright © 1969 by Holt, Rinehart and Winston, Inc.

The author's special thanks to Bruce Butte for his 31 illustrations signifying 31 years of 31 great ice cream flavors.

ISBN: 0-523-00754-X

First printing, November 1975

Cover illustration by Bruce Butte

Printed in the United States of America

PINNACLE BOOKS, INC.
275 Madison Avenue
New York, N. Y. 10016

ACKNOWLEDGMENTS

Irvine Robbins, Robert Hudecek, Bruce Enderwood, Art Rozell, Corris Guy and Marilyn Slack Novak.

And thanks to everyone else at Baskin-Robbins who so patiently put up with this project for such a very long time.

Cover and illustrations by Bruce Butte

CONTENTS

THE ICE CREAM WORLD
OF
BASKIN-ROBBINS

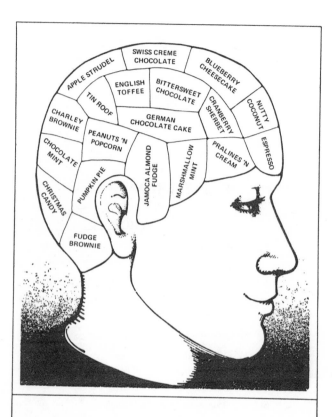

Think about ice cream and let your mind wander for a minute. If you're like most people, you'll quickly find yourself in a reverie of all things bright and beautiful. It's fantasy time when we think of ice cream because, throughout our lives, it has always been around when good things were happening. Birthday parties, baseball games, the circus, carnivals, picnics, field days, the last day of school. It's a symbol of happiness. It's magic.

And Baskin-Robbins has contributed more to that magic than anybody else in the world; just with flavors alone, Baskin-Robbins has made the ice cream fantasy more fantastic than ever and easier than ever for adults as well as kids to live the fantasy every day. Baskin-Robbins connoisseurs and fans (or fanatics, as the case may be) range from the super little to the superannuated—the smile of a person eating ice cream knows no age limitation. Ice cream is like a bouquet of flowers; it's a treat, something for a special occasion, a luxury item. It says, "Go ahead, indulge yourself a little. You deserve it, don't you?" And, if you're going to indulge, it might as well be Baskin-Robbins. It's the *best*.

Ice cream is, of itself, a particularly rewarding food. It is soft and easy to eat—it *literally* melts in your mouth. It is creamy, soothing, and cold, a combination of properties whose particular sensation is like no other. Think of the times your mother gave you ice cream when you were sick; it *soothed* you, made you feel better, while it nourished as well. If you ever had your tonsils out, we'll lay you a hundred to one the first thing the nurse brought you was a dish of vanilla ice cream. (Maybe it wasn't the best, but at that age who knew the difference as long as it was cold and smooth and slipped easily past all that pain in your throat.)

Besides its inherently pleasing qualities then, ice cream carries for us the strong connotation of pleasure, memories of happy times. Ice cream is an associational food, an impulse food, something magic, something to make us happy.

What, then, could be a better slogan for the world's largest ice cream company than *We Make People Happy*? Sound like an ego trip? Maybe at first it does, just a bit. "After all," you say, "who is some big company to proclaim that they make *me* happy?" It's very personal, but it also happens to be true. Because the great thing about Baskin-Robbins is that *they mean* it. From Irv Robbins and the late

20

Burton "Butch" Baskin on, Baskin-Robbins people are imbued with a spirit of dedication and loyalty to that principle of magic—*We Make People Happy*.

Sure, Baskin-Robbins is in business to make money. Who isn't? But the great thing is, it isn't just some big corporation making money. It's all those store owners out there with a personal, proprietary interest in their own share of "making people happy." That's the great concept of franchising. But that's business talk and this is an ice cream book.

During World War II, the men overseas dreamed a lot about the magic of ice cream; they longed for it because it represented everything positive and good about "Back Home"—the malt shop, the girlfriend waiting there (with apologies to the modern woman). Ice cream was a big thing during the war, a big symbol.

But then came a time when ice cream faded into a kind of oblivion, perhaps like everything else during the "Fabulous Fifties." Somebody came along and took away the magic.

The war ended and along came the fifties with their supermarkets and mass-produced, mass-marketed everything. Those great sodas and malts the soldiers had remembered so vividly were replaced by cartons of airy, bland, overstabilized "ice cream"—enough for every home to have some every night in front of that wondrous new marvel, the television. Drug store soda fountains were ripped out by the thousands, as proprietors realized they could make more money on other packaged items and not have to hassle with the "hang-out" crowd. This writer recalls the soda fountain at the Rexall Drug Store in Duxbury, Massachusetts. It was located at Hall's Corner (along with about six other stores, a law office, gas station, and Dodge dealer), and it had that incredible soda fountain smell—the sweet smell of syrup and soda combined with the pleasant dairy smell, the always-cool air, and the perfume counter on the other side of the store. That good old smell can still be found at, of all places, Schwab's Drug Store on Sunset Boulevard in Hollywood, not the actual one where Lana Turner wore her tight sweaters and sipped sodas, but close. It is a large, cool store with a fountain stretching the length of the right-hand wall. Beyond the fountain is a sit-down coffee shop where actors, directors, and such (some working, many not) talk loud show biz and pay exorbitant prices to be seen reading *Variety* and *The Hollywood Reporter*. Schwab's has that smell, that old feeling, and the great thing is, if you don't happen to think their ice cream measures up, you can walk around the corner to the Baskin-Robbins on Crescent Heights Boulevard.

So the fifties saw a pause in the magic. Cake mixes, TV dinners, packaged ice cream—anything easy was good. Who wanted to take time to bother with an extra step or an extra stop? If ice cream was available in the supermarkets, that was good enough. Nobody thought too much beyond quantity in the fifties.

Somebody did. In California, two pleasant young men were brewing up a potion that would create a renaissance of the ice cream magic as it had never before been known. By 1950, Baskin and Robbins were into their fifth year of business and operating around six ice cream stores in the Los Angeles area. They weren't yet known as Baskin-Robbins (some were called Burton's, some were known as Snowbird—it wasn't till '53 that Baskin-Robbins and the "31" concept got going). They always had lots and lots of flavors, though, and they concentrated on quality. They also were doing a few things nobody else seemed to think were important: they were hand packing their ice cream, they were giving some attention to the fountain business, and they were offering customers free tastes of the new, exotic flavors. Most important, they were specializing: they sold good ice cream, and that was it. No cigarettes, no potato chips, no sandwiches or coffee. It worked.

And the flavors worked. Pretty soon, Irv and Burt's business had gotten so big they contacted a fledgling ad agency, Carson/Roberts, and said they had a whopping $500 to do a "campaign." The young admen made a proposal which eventually cost considerably more (admen are known for this), but it was a winner. It involved "31 Flavors"—one for each day of the month—and a polka-dot theme: pink and brown, for cherry and chocolate, on a white ground, to symbolize the purity and cleanliness expected of all dairy products. Henceforth, all units would be referred to as Baskin-Robbins "31" Stores.

So ice cream as a treat, as something special, was on its way back to the American people, at least to the ones who lived in Southern California. Nobody, least of all Baskin and Robbins, had any idea it would blossom as it has.

Baskin and Robbins reinvented ice cream for America through their crazy, unique flavors and flavor names and their dedication to quality. They returned the magic to ice cream, made it fun and special again, and took it away from being just another frozen food in the supermarket. Sure, you can still buy half gallons and quarts and pints prepacked, but when you want the best ice cream, you can still get it—in enough incredible flavors to please the most particular palate. Baskin-Robbins has developed over four hundred, and those are just the ones that made it to the dipping cabinet! The list of suggestions is as endless as it is often preposterous.

This book contains recipes—and all of them use ice cream in some way or another. Baskin-Robbins has, without a doubt, done more for ice cream in the last two decades than anybody else had done since Nero sent his runners up to the mountains for ice to mix with fruit (we have it on somebody's authority that this is where "ice cream," or an iced confection, originated). One of the things Baskin-Robbins is trying to do is show people how to use ice cream in other concoctions, instead of just eating it off the end of a cone or out of a dish. Certainly ice cream, and particularly Baskin-Robbins ice cream, is great just by itself, but try a few of the recipes you find here and you'll realize it makes an amazingly versatile ingredient as well.

A great many of the recipes included in this book have come from you, the Baskin-Robbins fans. Nineteen seventy-three saw the first of the Baskin-Robbins Ice Cream Show Off Recipe Contests. Response was terrific, and many of the winning recipes were so good they have been included here. But the real stars of this book are the forty-six top-winning recipes from the 1975 Show Off. We have listed names of both 1973 and 1975 winners. Those recipes not credited have been developed by Baskin-Robbins under the supervision of Corris Guy, creative food consultant and home economist.

We have provided you with a whole year's worth of great ice cream dessert recipes to try. Pick your occasion, listed by month, and you'll find a special confection that will fit it perfectly. The recipes are interspersed with fun facts about ice cream and, of course, about Baskin-Robbins.

As long as Baskin-Robbins has brought the magic back to ice cream, you might as well be a real part of it. Read on!

The month of January was dedicated by the Romans to Janus, the two-headed god who presided over the entrance to the year, looking back to the year past and forward to the coming year at the same time. The Dutch used to call this month Lauwmaand (frosty month); the Saxons, Wulfmonath, since wolves were very troublesome then because of the scarcity of food. With the advent of Christianity the name was changed to Se aeftera geola (for after yule); it was also called Forma Monath (first month).

This is perfect. Beginning an ice cream recipe book on the first of January may do something to dispel the ugly rumor that ice cream is primarily a summertime treat. Well, it isn't, and the mere existence of a company like Baskin-Robbins in climates from New York to Tokyo is proof enough of that. Ice cream is great the year 'round as you, the reader and connoisseur of ice cream, undoubtedly already know. To an ice cream freak there is no season.

Pralines 'n Cream is the same great stuff whether you're enjoying it on a stroll through Central Park in August or while you're watching the Rose Bowl game on New Year's Day. As Irv Robbins says, "It's always summertime in your living room."

If you acted like the typical carousing fool the night before, however, New Year's morning may not be quite so summery. But it's a holiday, so relax. There's nothing to do but sit around and watch the parade, a game or two, maybe read a little, or invite friends over. Just in case things did get a little out of hand the night before, skip the Bloody Mary and start the New Year right with our ice cream-Kahlua concoction. What could be more soothing? By the time the Baskin-Robbins Rose Parade float has crossed your TV screen, things will seem a great deal more pleasant. Ice cream has that effect on people (with a little help from the Kahlua).

January can be a letdown time for some: the holiday season has passed, and though many people profess loudly that they would be happier never to see another December holiday, that the whole thing is a big waste of time and effort, they still feel (and probably secretly enjoy) the hustle and bustle that surrounds the festive season. So when it's all over, even die-hard Scrooges are bound to experience some sense of letdown, if only in the moods of their friends.

Cold January is a time of reality. The holiday

fantasies are over—times when people got together to renew or extend friendships, times when charity seemed to broaden, times when dieters threw fate to the wind and indulged in that extra piece of pie. January is resolution time. The weather's not good, end-of-last-year bills mount up, taxes loom in a few months, the flu hits, business is down. It always takes a while to get the year going properly.

So while you're maintaining your new belt-tightening program as strictly as possible, don't be too hard on yourself in January. Let go just a bit, and the month will go by in great style. Give a January doldrum party and whip up something like the Kahlua Delight offered on page 42. That'll cure the blues. And for cold days we've given you a few hot drinks to improve the grouchiest mood. When you think about it, January is a great month for ice cream! What better time to treat yourself and your friends to the world's most soothing confection?

New Year's Day

If you do get up and things don't set so well between the old eyes, don't waste time feeling guilty about last night. After all, it *was* New Year's Eve; so what if you made a fool of yourself? Sit down and have a look at the Tournament of Roses

Parade—your favorite ice cream company's got a float in it. Before you get too comfortable, though, there's something you ought to try. It's a cross between a drink and a sundae, and it combines Jamoca ice cream with eggnog and Kahlua. Go ahead, do it! Treat yourself. And Happy New Year from Baskin-Robbins!

NEW YEAR'S KAHLUA KURE

½ pint whipping cream, whipped

1 quart Baskin-Robbins Jamoca® Ice Cream

¼ cup Kahlua

1 cup chilled dairy eggnog

Chocolate shavings, optional

Reserve ½ cup whipped cream for garnish. Divide remaining whipped cream between 4 to 5 tall glasses; top each with 2 scoops of ice cream. Combine eggnog and Kahlua; pour over ice cream in glasses. Garnish with reserved cream and chocolate shavings, if desired. Makes 4 to 5 servings.

Juell Vishnesky, St. Louis County, Missouri (1975)

New Year's is a time to try something different, so we're offering you this special prize-winning sundae with an exotic blend of nuts, raisins, cinnamon, chocolate, and coffee flavors. It's a whole new taste experience, worthy of the first day of a great new year.

NEW YEAR'S SUNDAE

½ cup chopped walnuts	1 jar (9 ounces) Baskin-Robbins Hot Fudge
½ cup chopped raisins	
2 teaspoons cinnamon	1 quart Baskin-Robbins Jamoca® Ice Cream
4 teaspoons sugar	

Mix nuts, raisins, cinnamon, and sugar in a small bowl. Gently heat hot fudge sauce; scoop ice cream into dessert dishes. Top each with fudge sauce, then sprinkle with nut-raisin mixture. (If desired, top with whipped cream and a cherry.) Makes 8 servings.

Norma Taylor, Eugene, Oregon (1975)

CITRUS CAPRICORN

Capricorns—safe, middle-ground people with an uncanny will—enjoy this simple, light dessert. It's just enough to satisfy, yet not enough to overfill. It's a great blend of tangy citrus with creamy citrus, the perfect end to any substantial meal.

1 cup orange juice	¼ cup cold water
1½ tablespoons lemon juice	1 quart Baskin-Robbins Fresh Peach Ice Cream
⅓ cup sugar	
1 teaspoon grated orange peel	1 quart Baskin-Robbins Orange Sherbet
1 tablespoon cornstarch	Lemon twists, optional

Mix first four ingredients together in a saucepan. Mix cornstarch to a smooth consistency in cold water. Stir into orange juice mixture. Bring just to a boil, stirring constantly. When thickened slightly, remove from heat. Place one scoop each of ice cream and sherbet in each of six sundae or elongated dessert dishes. Spoon warm sauce over all; top with a lemon twist. Makes 6 servings.

Candice B. Biggs, Dayton, Ohio (1973)

Alaska Admission Day

On January 3, 1959, Alaska became the 49th state and replaced the braggart Texas as the nation's largest. In honor of that historic event, we present a fudgy variation on baked Alaska, for years an American favorite.

INDIVIDUAL BROWNIE ALASKAS

1 package fudge brownie mix
4 egg whites
½ cup sugar

1 pint Baskin-Robbins Chocolate Almond Ice Cream

Bake mix according to directions on package. Cut into 3-inch squares. Cool, chill. Top each square with small scoop of ice cream. Place on baking sheet. Freeze for at least 1 hour. Preheat oven to 450 degrees. Beat egg whites until foamy; beat in sugar, 1 tablespoon at a time. Continue beating until stiff and glossy. Cover brownies and ice cream with meringue, sealing it to edge of brownies. Bake about 4 minutes or until meringue is a delicate brown. Serve immediately. Makes 9 servings.

The Battle of New Orleans

The Battle of New Orleans, a paper tiger battle really, was fought on January 8, 1815, part of the War of 1812. While the Americans had already won and the peace treaty had been signed, the battle was bloodily fought and stupidly lost at great expense to the British. According to the *Oxford History of the American People*, "... it made a future president of the United States, and in folklore wiped out all previous American defeats, ending the 'Second War of Independence' in a blaze of glory." The future president was Andrew Jackson. As a tribute to American folklore and the ever-present system of politics, we offer a superior Battle of New Orleans Parfait.

NEW ORLEANS FRENCH PARFAIT

3 tablespoons butter	1 quart Baskin-Robbins Butter Pecan or French Vanilla Ice Cream
1¼ cups chopped pecans	
½ cup Baskin-Robbins Butterscotch Topping	
1 tablespoon vanilla	Whipped topping, optional

Melt butter in small skillet; stir in 1 cup of the pecans and cook over low heat for 5 minutes. Add butterscotch topping and vanilla; cook, stirring, until heated through. Cool. Layer ice cream and pecan mixture into each of four parfait glasses. Top, if desired, with whipped topping and remaining chopped pecans. Makes 4 servings.

Elin A. Hawkins, Glendale, Arizona (1973)

A Tale of 31 Roses

Baskin-Robbins has become a colorful and creative fixture in the annual Tournament of Roses Parade. Over the past several years national audiences have seen the world's greatest smiling, flower-covered clown, the most incredible, and only, oval carousel ever devised, and the biggest scale Model T known to man.

The first Rose Parade entry portrayed the Baskin-Robbins spirit with a massive laughing clown whose costume sported 31 balloons (representing scoops, naturally), each covered with thousands of its own special variety of rose—31 "scoop" shapes, 31 kinds of roses. The clown design featured the greatest variety of roses ever used on any float in the history of the Rose Parade and won the President's Trophy for the most effective use of roses.

The second entry was a mechanical wonder. Who ever heard of an oval carousel propelling itself along Colorado Boulevard? The fanciful merry-go-round had 31 riders, each made up to represent an animal caricature, all covered with seeds, flowers, and other organic material (nothing used to adorn a Rose Parade float can be synthetic). The caricatures moved around the structure and up and down as the entire unit drove along the street. Probably one of the most original floats ever designed, the "oval-go-round" won the Mayor's Trophy that year—1974.

The Model T year was 1975, and never has a float so authentically represented anything. The car was a scale replica, totally adorned with flowers and other natural materials, which actually operated under its own power on its own four huge wheels (this 6′6″ author couldn't see eye-to-eye with the top of the petal-covered wheels).

Most floats are just that—"floats" which sort of drift down the boulevard. This grand entry actually motored along all by itself, complete with its larger-than-life American family members, straight out of 1909. The day before the parade, those brave souls who donned the costumes spent many a traumatic minute rehearsing the climb into that jumbo vehicle. Their papier-mâché heads alone stood as tall as many of the volunteer students working on the final preparation of the floats.

The greatest Baskin-Robbins Rose Parade story,

however, took place quite a few years ago, when the "Rover Boys" (as Baskin and Robbins were called by their long-time advertising agent and friend Ralph Carson) had the idea to capitalize on the captive crowd lined up on Colorado Boulevard on January 1. The year was, let's say, 1947.

The ice cream duo had some novelties—chocolate-covered bars and the like—made up and packaged, found some teenagers to hawk them, and rented a station wagon from which to supply the individual vendors. Fine. Great idea. Except they discovered they had to obtain permits for each of the kids (ten bucks apiece). But they figured they'd make so much money on sales and gain such great publicity it would all be worth it.

They had the station wagon painted with water-soluble paint, loaded it up, and somehow managed to park it, full of the ice cream goodies, near the stands along Colorado.

The morning of the parade was cold and windy. For some reason nobody wanted ice cream, particularly at 25¢ a pop, so the price went gradually down. After it reached a nickel with still no takers, the disheartened Baskin and Robbins made a final attempt to recoup by renting the roof of their already-rented wagon to a newsreel cameraman, who found it a perfect vantage point. They charged him $25.00, which would have been fine if his camera tripod hadn't torn a hole in the roof. "After we paid to repair the roof and have the entire car repainted (the paint, it turned out, was not as soluble as its manufacturer had promised), we had about $50.00 left between us," Robbins recalls. Twenty-five years later it must have given "Horatio Alger" Robbins a pretty special thrill to see his own company's $40,-000 float brightening the New Year's morning of millions on national television.

•   •   •

A lot of people have probably wondered just how those massive New Year's Day floats are made. And maybe just as many have thought the whole thing is a big waste of time, money, and energy in a world where so many important things are neglected. But if you think of the Rose Parade as an entertainment, a bang-up, positive way to start a new year (not to mention a nice pastime for anybody with a hangover), it doesn't seem quite so extravagant. Broadway shows cost a lot of money, movies cost more, and think of the dollars spent on Vegas extravaganzas! And besides entertaining all those people, the Rose Parade is an incredible advertising medium for companies like Baskin-Robbins. Estimates of the value of air time run into hundreds of thousands of dollars. It seems incredible, but there are four major companies whose sole function it is to design, engineer, construct, and decorate floats—not just for the Rose Parade but also for other parades and pageants. Festival Artists has brought into being each of the ice cream floats, all of which have won major prizes.

The process begins early in the year, usually in the beginning of April, when Festival Artists designers present Baskin-Robbins with several different concepts, all relating to the parade theme. Once one is selected, work begins immediately in Festival Artists' hangarlike buildings opposite the Rose Bowl in Pasadena. It's like setting out to build a big building—that much engineering goes into making an oval carousel turn and bob at the same time or getting a giant Model T to function under its own power.

Most of the major float companies execute about ten floats for each parade (a lot of the noncommercial entries are done by private volunteer groups). By the beginning of December the Festival Artists quarters are a madhouse, and the builders are just about mad. Massive, ugly metal structures loom up to the ceiling, blow torches light the room, and nothing looks even remotely ready. There isn't a flower in sight, and although people are hard at work, there never seems to be enough of them to get it all done in time. But the day after Christmas the place begins to fill up, the flowers start arriving, and somehow those ugly masses of metal are transformed into the famous floats. Kids from churches and philanthropic organizations are assigned to each float (the float builder pays the organization, and the kids donate their time). Flowers, seeds, leaves, petals, grass—anything organic can be used to adorn a float, and the least perishable go on first. Areas are periodically covered with cheesecloth and sprayed to maintain vitality, and it isn't till the last day or two that actual whole roses, orchids, carnations, and other flowers are added, each in its little water-filled test-tube-like vase. Suddenly the floats take on star quality—people want to get near them and touch them. TV news crews arrive to tape specials, and a long catwalk above the whole scene of floral bedlam fills up with intrigued spectators.

Finally the decoration is completed, and the float builders' only worry now is whether all the mechanical ingenuity they built into their designs is going to withstand the actual stress of the parade route. Are all those mechanized heads going to turn, platforms revolve, engines keep running? It's a gamble, because any float that breaks down during the parade has just about one minute to get moving again, or strategically placed towtrucks come and help it along (not exactly the best P.R. on national television).

So far, Baskin-Robbins' floats have been absolute perfection, but what would you expect from the people who make the world's greatest ice cream?

• • •

Here's a great dessert combination of cherry and chocolate, specially designed to cheer the depression out of the coldest, dankest January night. It's simple, too.

40

CORDIALLY YOURS

1 pint Baskin-Robbins Chocolate Fudge Ice Cream	4 maraschino cherries with stems
4 jiggers Cheri-Suisse Liqueur	4 tablespoons brandy Confectioners' sugar

Marinate cherries in brandy for at least 2 hours. Dip rims of champagne glasses (not hollow stem) in water in a saucer, then into confectioners' sugar. Place in freezer for at least 20 minutes. To serve, place scoop of ice cream into each chilled, frosted champagne glass. Pour liqueur over each scoop; top with brandied cherry. Makes 4 servings.

Anita Diggle, New York City (1973)

Prohibition Day

On January 16, 1920, the Congress of the United States ratified the 18th Amendment to the Constitution, outlawing the use, sale, or distribution of alcoholic beverages. While most now agree that this was folly, since it promoted an increase in organized crime, it just happened to be a boon to the ice cream industry. Those men who were unable to obtain bootleg whiskey were much more apt to stop on their way home to pick up some ice cream for the family, whereas previously they would have stopped for a quick snort. Ice cream, being nearly as addictive as alcohol, became much more popular during Prohibition. As mentioned in the introductory passage to this chapter, we offer a delightfully sinful recipe both to scorn the passage of the prohibition law and to perk up any January party. The virtue of Kahlua Delight has nothing to do with the alcohol: it's simply an incredible recipe.

Baskin Banshee, the second recipe for Prohibition day, is a coffee-banana combination that'll give your eyeballs a twinge. In this case, the liquor definitely makes a difference. Happy sailing!

KAHLUA DELIGHT

1 quart Baskin-Robbins   Whipped Cream Topping
    Jamoca® Ice Cream   (recipe follows)
1 Kahlua Fudge Cake

Slightly soften ice cream; spread evenly in a foil-lined 9-inch layer cake pan. Freeze until firm, about 3 hours. Meanwhile, bake cake layers; cool, chill. To assemble, place one cake layer on serving plate; top with ice cream layer, then with second cake layer. Frost sides and top with whipped cream topping. Serve immediately or freeze, uncovered, until whipped cream is firm, then cover; freeze at least 3 hours. To serve frozen, let mellow at room temperature for about 10 minutes before cutting. Makes 12 servings.

Kahlua Fudge Cake

1 package (16 ounces) pound cake mix
1 package (15.4 ounces) fudge frosting mix
2 teaspoons cinnamon
¼ teaspoon cloves
½ cup double-strength coffee (2 teaspoons instant coffee, ½ cup water)
1 cup dairy sour cream
2 eggs
1 teaspoon grated orange peel
½ cup chopped nuts
¼ cup sugar
2 tablespoons hot double-strength coffee
4 tablespoons Kahlua

Preheat oven to 325 degrees. Grease and flour 2 round 9-inch cake pans. Combine the first 4 ingredients in a large mixing bowl; stir in the ½ cup coffee and sour cream. Blend until dry ingredients are moistened, then beat one minute on mixer's medium speed (or 150 hand strokes). Scrape bowl and beater, add eggs, and blend well. Beat 2 minutes on medium speed; stir in orange peel. Pour batter into prepared pans; sprinkle with nuts. Bake 40 minutes at 325 degrees or until done. Just before cake is done, dissolve the sugar in the 2 tablespoons of coffee and stir in Kahlua. Remove cake layers from oven and cool slightly in pan. Turn out onto cooling racks. Puncture tops in many places with a fork. Slowly spoon syrup over each layer, allowing cake to absorb syrup. Chill layers.

Whipped Cream Topping

Whip 1 pint heavy or whipping cream until stiff peaks form, adding 1 to 2 tablespoons of sugar. Fold in 2 tablespoons Kahlua and 1 teaspoon vanilla. Refrigerate until ready to use.

Erin Cleveland, Sacramento, California (1975)

BASKIN BANSHEE

3 tablespoons creme de banana

3 tablespoons creme de cacao

1 pint Baskin-Robbins Banana Marshmallow Ice Cream, slightly softened

Mix ingredients just until blended in blender or mixer. Serve, with a spoon, in champagne glasses or demitasse cups. Makes 4 to 5 servings.

Frances G. Morris, Tucker, Georgia (1975)

This variation on coffee is as easy as instant and as good as the finest Capuccino.

HOT ROBBINS

¼ cup instant coffee
¼ cup sugar
1 tablespoon cinnamon
1 tablespoon nutmeg
6 cups boiling water

1 quart Baskin-Robbins
    Jamoca® Ice Cream
Whipped cream or topping
Cinnamon

Mix together the instant coffee, sugar, cinnamon, and nutmeg. Store in tightly covered container. To serve, place 1 tablespoon of the coffee-sugar mixture into each large coffee mug. Pour boiling water into mugs, filling two-thirds full. Add 1 scoop ice cream to each mug; top each with whipped cream and a sprinkle of cinnamon. Serve immediately. Makes 8 to 10 servings.

Mr. and Mrs. Randy J. Powell, Prescott, Arizona
(1975)

Of Bowls Not Full of Roses . . .

You can bet that if roses somehow could have been made into a palatable ice cream, Baskin-Robbins would have done it by now and there would be twenty different rose variations, plus hundreds of suggestions for special desserts honoring the Rose Bowl. But alas, rose ice cream seems to be impossible. Not so with the orange.

45

Orange season and the Orange Bowl rate some special attention, so Florida fans, get ready! Two special recipes follow just for you.

SPICY ORANGE ZEBRA

Off the beaten path from Cleveland, Ohio, there's a somewhat bizarre but generally pretty excellent institution of higher learning called Oberlin College. During the sixties, the college food service offered as a special treat a dessert called Zebra Cake. It consisted of chocolate ice-box cookies layered with whipped cream and allowed to get soggy in the refrigerator. This Spicy Orange Zebra is another delightful variation on that popular dessert. Perhaps Thayer Hopkins, creator of the variation, attended a school where the original Zebra Cake was served.

3 oranges	¼ cup sugar
15 thin ginger cookies, ½″ thick (or other flavor)	1 teaspoon ginger
	½ teaspoon cinnamon
1 quart Baskin-Robbins French Vanilla Ice Cream	1 cup whipping or heavy cream
	½ cup triple sec liqueur

(Grate and reserve 2 teaspoons of orange peel. Peel 2 of the oranges; cut six ½″ slices. Reserve third orange for garnish.) Pour triple sec over orange slices; let marinate about 3 hours. Take 6 cookies and spread each with about ½ cup of ice cream. Top each ice-cream-covered cookie with a second cookie, making 6 ice cream sandwiches. Freeze. Drain orange slices, reserving triple sec liquid. Place orange slices on waxed paper; chill in freezer. When ice cream in sandwiches is firm, remove one sandwich at a time from freezer. Smooth about 1 tablespoon of ice cream on top of each sandwich; return to freezer. Take the 3 remaining cookies; spread one side of each with 1 tablespoon of ice cream. Freeze at least 2 hours. Make 3 cookie stacks. Take one ice cream sandwich, cookie side down; top with an orange slice. Place a second ice cream sandwich on top of the orange slice, cookie side up. Spread 1 tablespoon ice cream on top of last cookie; add another orange slice. End with one of the 3 single cookies, placing ice cream side down. Place stack in freezer. Repeat process two more times to make 3 cookie stacks, using all cookies, ice cream, and orange slices. Combine sugar, the 2 teaspoons of grated orange peel, ginger, cinnamon, and ¼ cup of the liquid drained from oranges. Whip cream just until it holds its shape; whip in sugar-spice liquid. Lay the 3 cookie stacks side by side (not end to end) on edge, on a serving plate. Frost whole dessert with whipped cream mixture. Garnish with thin half-slices from the third orange. Freeze at least 4 hours. Allow dessert to mellow about 15 minutes in refrigerator before slicing crosswise into servings. Makes 9 servings.

Thayer Hopkins, Jr., Providence, Rhode Island
(1975)

ICE CREAM A L'ORANGE

4 large oranges
6 tablespoons Cointreau
  (or other orange
  liqueur)
1 quart Baskin-Robbins
  Fresh Banana, French

Vanilla, or Chocolate
  Chip Ice Cream
6 tablespoons finely
  chopped walnuts
6 fresh mint sprigs, op-
  tional

Finely grate enough orange peel to make 6 table-spoons. Peel oranges and slice, crosswise, into thin slices; cut into bite-size pieces. Line the bottom of 6 individual dessert dishes with the orange pieces. Drizzle 2 teaspoons of Cointreau over each serving. Place a large scoop of ice cream in the center of each dish. Drizzle each scoop with a teaspoon of Cointreau; sprinkle with 1 tablespoon each of wal-nuts and grated orange peel. Garnish, if desired, with mint sprigs. Makes 6 servings.

Kim DuClair, San Leandro, California (1975)

"STEVERINO"

When friends Irv Robbins and Burt Baskin kiddingly challenged Steve Allen to come up with a flavor utilizing his favorite ingredients, he called their bluff and created a national stir (and lots of publicity for Baskin-Robbins) by working out the flavor on the air. From 48 ingredients made available to him Steve picked pistachio nuts, fresh coconut, strawberries, maraschino cherries, cashews, fresh plums, peaches, pears, boysenberries, and fern candy (fudge chip). Sounds terrible, but somebody must have liked it: "Steverino" sold over 1,000,000 scoops in its first month.

What's February got to offer? Well, it has Groundhog Day, it has Lincoln's and Washington's birthdays, it has Valentine's Day, and it has rain or snow. There is skiing if you're lucky, just plain cold and wet if you're not. For some people, February means cruises to the Caribbean or gilt-edged vacations in Miami Beach or Palm Springs. February is the month when, by all rights, winter should end, and it doesn't. It is kind of hard to recall much about February; after all, it is only 28 days long, and that always comes as a surprise. Even for those who live in the cold climates there isn't much to remember about this month—it's kind of an extension of January, except there is no traditional "thaw" at the end. February is, you might say, the "dead" of winter.

So we've perked it up for you with lots of great recipes, including two special New Orleans treats honoring Mardi Gras. If you can't make it down to the mouth of the old Mississippi for the festivities, stage your own revelry at home and make sure one of these classic desserts is a major part of it. Mardi Gras is one of February's real highs, so make the most of it.

February is also National Cherry Month, according to the National Cherry Institute. Since it is hardly cherry season, one assumes the idea is to honor George Washington's cherry tree experience—and what more appropriate time than on his birthday? In honor of Honest George and his cherry tree, we have provided you with three scrumptious recipes, using, among many other things, Baskin-Robbins Burgundy Cherry Ice Cream, which, like canned cherries, just happens to be available year 'round.

Aquarius

Aquarians love surprises, even little ones, so give yours a start with ice-cream-filled cupcakes—perfect for the mini-Aquarian's birthday party.

GERMAN CHOCOLATE SURPRISES

1 package (18.5 ounces) chocolate cake mix
1 package (9.9 ounces) coconut pecan frosting mix

1 quart Baskin-Robbins Coconut Chocolate Chip or Coconut Almond Fudge Ice Cream

Prepare cake batter according to package directions. Spoon batter into 18 large paper baking cups in a muffin tin or greased custard cups. Bake according to package directions. Cool. Make a large cavity in the center of each cupcake, leaving sides and bottom intact. Put cupcakes in freezer. Make frosting according to package directions. Cool. Fill cupcake cavities with ice cream level with top. Frost thickly with cooled frosting, making sure ice cream is well covered. Freeze. Just before serving, put cupcakes under broiler *just* until topping starts to bubble. Serve immediately. Makes 18 servings.

Linda Buddenberg, San Marino, California
(1975)

Groundhog Day

On Candlemas, February second, Groundhog Day, our burrowing friend comes out of his hole for the first time. As we know, we don't want him to see his shadow, as that means he will return to his hole for another six weeks, bringing six more weeks of foul weather. Lure him away with this delicious and irresistible Mud Pie; he'll be so busy eating he won't have time to look at any old shadow.

MUD PIE

1⅓ cups chocolate wafer crumbs
3 tablespoons soft butter
1 quart Chocolate Fudge Ice Cream
1 pint Bavarian Choclate Mint Ice Cream

Mix crumbs and butter until crumbly. Press to bottom and sides of 9-inch pie plate. Bake at 375 degrees for 8 minutes. Cool, chill. Slightly soften Chocolate Fudge Ice Cream. Spread over crust, mounding in center. Spread slightly softened Bavarian Ice Cream over Chocolate Fudge, texturing surface with spoon. Freeze at least 2 hours. Makes 10 generous servings.

The Scoop on Scoops

Wouldn't it seem that something as apparently simple as an ice cream scoop should have a short and simple history? Not so, not so at all. Since they started wrapping waffles into cones and plopping ice cream on top way back at the St. Louis exposition in 1904, there have been just about as many scoop variations as Baskin-Robbins flavors, many of them actually developed by Baskin-Robbins.

For quite a few years Baskin-Robbins stores were just like all the rest with their scoops—you took what you could get, and sometimes you didn't get as much as the next fella. Scoops varied from store to store, and it was always Burt Baskin's dream to develop a completely standard, unique Baskin-Robbins scoop which, when properly handled, would dispense equal portions of ice cream to each customer. After all, what parent needs Johnnie crying because Janie got more ice cream in her cone? (Knowing how possessive some of our adult ice cream freaks can get, there might be some scenes on that level as well.)

Baskin in 1964 commissioned a dedicated ally to the task of coming up with the ultimate scoop, exclusive for Baskin-Robbins. It wasn't until late 1969 that the job had been completed—at an estimated cost of around 1,600 person hours—and something similar to the scoop you see today in Baskin-Robbins stores was in use. But that didn't last long:

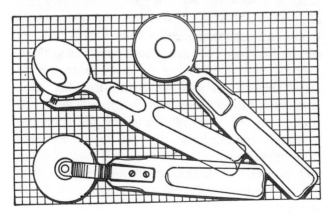

the company with whom they had signed an exclusive contract to produce the scoops went bust, and Baskin-Robbins was left holding not enough scoops. Another manufacturer has of course been found, and it seems that things will remain pretty solid in the scoop department for a while.

The reasons for all this turmoil are many. First, as mentioned, the scoop must be designed so that when it is rolled around a tub of ice cream in the way all Baskin-Robbins employees are trained to use it, it will produce a ball of ice cream which is just that: a ball, and an attractive, neat-looking one which, if weighed, would be precisely 2.5 ounces. Second, Baskin-Robbins has stores in many different cities with many different types of water; since the scoop must spend a great deal of its time sitting in water (although the less time the better from the point of view of the store owner), it must be made of an alloy which resists corroding and pitting of all types, not just those peculiar to one area. This, as can be imagined, is a tall order. People who think they can manufacture just the right scoop are always sending samples to Baskin-Robbins. One company's model seemed to fit the bill very well back in the 60's when all this testing was going on, so Baskin commissioned it to use in the company store in Burbank. After three days it was so pitted and corroded it looked as though it had gone around the world attached to the stern of a tramp steamer.

But the alloy problem was solved, and scoop development moved into its most critical area. It seemed that to come up with just the right curves in just the right places to scoop out just the right amount of ice cream, Baskin and Robbins had to employ the art of lost wax casting, in existence since Biblical times, an art which since the days of Francois Auguste Rodin has been indulged in primarily by manufacturers of intricate parts for aircraft and other sophisticated machinery. As in Rodin's time, the process involves the shaping or sculpting of a wax mold to exactly represent the finished product; this mold is then set on a "tree" with a group of others just like it and dipped in a succession of about ten solutions, including sand, gravel and paste, and each dipping is given plenty of time to dry. Finally the whole contraption is heated, the wax melts and drips out, and there's your casting—an elaborate, glazed ceramic tree. The molten steel alloy is poured into this and allowed to dry and cure, or temper. Then a man comes along with a sledgehammer, gives it a whack, and there you have them, the pieces that will make up the scoops. The several pieces are welded together, polished, and sent out to perform their all-important task in Baskin-Robbins stores.

All that work for a lousy ice cream scoop, you say? But the end result is practically indestructible, it is unique, and it performs all the functions Burt

Baskin required of it when he set its development into motion over ten years ago.

Remember the Boy Scouts

On February 8, 1910, General Sir Robert Baden-Powell organized a group of boys for the purpose of strengthening principles of good citizenship, service to others, cleanliness, and self-reliance, all based primarily on training in an outdoor setting. The movement became world-wide and currently has a membership of over eight million young people. Whether you once were a Boy Scout yourself, are married to someone who was, or have your own scout running around the house, this All-American Apple Tart recipe is intended for you. It tops apple pie a la mode! And what all-American boy would turn that down?

ALL-AMERICAN APPLE TARTS

1 pint Baskin-Robbins French Vanilla Ice Cream
2 teaspoons apple pie spice (or 1 teaspoon *each* nutmeg and cinnamon)
5 baked pie-crust tart shells (4″ diameter)

1 cup Granola cereal
2 tablespoons butter or margarine, softened
1¼ cups shredded Cheddar cheese
1 can (1 pound, 5 ounces) prepared apple pie filling

Make 5 scoops of ice cream; put on tray, freeze until firm. Mix apple pie spice into apple pie filling; set aside. Lightly mix remaining ingredients, except tarts, until crumbly. In each tart shell, place a heaping tablespoonful of spiced pie filling. Top each with a scoop of ice cream. Spoon on remaining pie filling, covering ice cream in each tart. Sprinkle each tart with the Granola-cheese mixture, covering top generously. Freeze at least one hour. To serve, set oven control at broil. Place tarts on pan or board, place 4 inches from heat; broil about 1 minute or until topping is puffy and bubbly. Serve immediately. Makes 5 servings.

Esther Ott, Bellevue, Washington (1973)

Abraham Lincoln's Birthday

If ever the United States had a President who truly understood the meaning of democracy and the responsibility it implies for every citizen, it was Abraham Lincoln. Reflect on a few of his words:

> "I go for all sharing the privileges of the government who assist in bearing its burdens."

59

"If destruction be our lot we must ourselves be its author and finisher. As a nation of free men we must live through all time, or die by suicide."

"There is no grievance that is a fit object of redress by mob law."

"No man is good enough to govern another man without that other's consent."

"The ballot is stronger than the bullet."

"As I would not be a slave, so I would not be a master. This expresses my idea of democracy. Whatever differs from this, to the extent of the difference, is no democracy."

Although Abraham Lincoln has been dead well over a hundred years, it is still possible to relate almost personally to his great pragmatic, honest wisdom through his many recorded words. Maybe each of us should stop for a minute this year on Lincoln's birthday and consider it more than just another day off (which in most cases it isn't anyway—and Lincoln would have wanted it that way). Very often we become so preoccupied with the leisure time any holiday provides us that we lose sight of what it is we're supposed to be commemorating.

LEMON GINGERBREAD LINCOLN LOG

¾ cup all-purpose flour
½ teaspoon *each* salt, baking powder, baking soda, ginger
1 quart Baskin-Robbins Lemon Custard Ice Cream

4 eggs
½ cup sugar
½ cup molasses
Confectioners' sugar
¼ teaspoon *each* cloves, allspice

Heat oven to 375 degrees. Line jelly roll pan, 15" × 10" × 1", with waxed paper or foil; grease. (Or, line pan with paper toweling; do not grease.) Sift flour, salt, baking powder and soda, and spices together. Beat eggs until very thick and lemon colored, about 5 minutes; gradually beat in sugar. On low speed blend in molasses; gradually add sifted dry ingredients, beating just until batter is smooth. Pour into lined pan, spreading batter to corners. Bake 12 to 15 minutes, or until wooden pick inserted in center comes out clean. Loosen cake from edges of pan; invert on towel sprinkled with confectioners' sugar. Carefully remove paper or foil; trim off stiff edges if necessary. While hot, roll cake and towel from narrow end. Cool on wire rack. Unroll cake, spread with slightly softened Lemon Custard Ice Cream or any other Baskin-Robbins lemon-flavored ice cream. Roll up; sprinkle with confectioners' sugar. Lay on chilled serving plate. Freeze at least 2 hours. Makes 10 servings.

Mary Cassel, Tulsa, Oklahoma (1973)

Valentine's Day

Since the National Date Festival (you can decide whether that means the kind of date you eat or the kind you kiss good night) happens to coincide with St. Valentine's Day, we offer you Double-Date Sundae, a great variation on date bread with cream cheese that happens to suit both occasions.

And for Valentine's Day alone there is a really unique concoction, one of several submitted to the recipe contest combining avocados with ice cream. In this case it's quite simple, but the result is like nothing you've ever tasted. They're called California Love Cups because the Avocado Growers Association has called its product "Love Food From California." We don't mind giving them a little plug—avocados are kind of like Baskin-Robbins ice cream—a hard thing to dislike.

DOUBLE-DATE SUNDAE

6 slices (½-inch thick) date-nut bread	1 jar (9¾ ounces) Baskin-Robbins Butterscotch Topping, warmed
1 package (3 ounces) cream cheese, softened	6 pecan-stuffed dates
1 pint Baskin-Robbins Butter Pecan Ice Cream	

Spread the date-nut bread slices with softened cream cheese. Place each slice in a shallow dessert dish or compote. Top each with a large scoop of ice cream. Spoon the warm sauce over each scoop. Top with a pecan-stuffed date. Makes 6 servings.

Ellen B. Friedman, Beachwood, Ohio (1975)

CALIFORNIA LOVE CUPS

1¼ cups graham cracker
    crumbs
¼ cup sugar
½ teaspoon cinnamon
2 tablespoons toasted
    sesame seeds
¼ cup softened butter or
    margarine

1 quart Baskin-Robbins
    Lemon Custard or
    French Vanilla Ice
    Cream
Paper baking cups
1 recipe Lime Love Top-
    ping (recipe follows)

In a medium bowl combine crumbs, sugar, cinnamon, and sesame seeds. Add butter; blend well with fork or fingers. Store in plastic bag or jar. Refrigerate. Scoop 10 large balls of ice cream and place in freezer on a baking sheet. Place paper baking cups in a muffin tin. Working with a few scoops at a time, roll in crumb mixture and place in baking cups. Freeze until solid.

Lime Love Topping

In blender, put ¼ cup lime juice, 1 can sweetened condensed milk (14 ounces, not evaporated), and 1 ripe avocado, peeled and cut in chunks. Blend on medium high speed just until smooth and velvety. Refrigerate. Makes 2½ cups. At serving time, remove balls from freezer. Peel off paper and place in serving dishes. Top each with 1 tablespoon Lime Love Topping. Garnish with additional crumbs and slice of lime, if desired. Makes 10 servings.

Bonnie Sue Schneider, Scotts Valley, California
(1975)

Burgundy Cherry

While Burgundy Cherry may not be a Baskin-Robbins exclusive, it is most definitely a favorite. Almost from the time of its introduction in Baskin-Robbins stores back in the 1950's it has been a "regular" flavor, meaning it is available twelve months of the year. Its great popularity may be attributed to the fact that it uses dark, rich, and juicy bing cherries instead of the bright red maraschinos that often taste like plastic. Obviously, its popularity has not waned, since an enormous proportion of entries in the 1975 Show Off made use of it in one way or another. We have picked three of the best recipes and offer them to help you celebrate both George Washington's Birthday and National Cherry Month.

BURGUNDY CHERRY-CHEESE PIE

2 packages (3 ounces)
    cream cheese
⅓ cup sugar
1 teaspoon vanilla
1 cup whipping cream

2 tablespoons sugar
1 9-inch baked pie crust
1 quart Baskin-Robbins
    Burgundy Cherry
    Ice Cream

Cream cheese and ⅓ cup sugar together until smooth; add vanilla and blend well. In medium bowl, whip cream with 2 tablespoons sugar just until stiff. Fold whipped cream into cream cheese mixture. Spoon into pie crust. Freeze at least 1 hour. Top pie with slightly softened ice cream. Freeze at least 2 hours. Allow to mellow in refrigerator for 10 minutes before serving. Makes 6 servings.

Sandi Bledsoe, Austin, Texas (1973)

FROZEN BLACK FOREST TORTE

1 quart Baskin-Robbins Burgundy Cherry Ice Cream
¾ cup chocolate cherry liqueur (or Cheri-Suisse)
1 pint Baskin-Robbins French Vanilla Ice Cream
1 package (18½ ounces) sour cream chocolate fudge cake mix
½ cup chopped nuts, optional
1 pint whipping or heavy cream, whipped, sweetened
Chocolate curls
1 can (8¾ ounces) black cherries, thoroughly drained

Line three round 8-inch cake pans with plastic wrap. Slightly soften the Burgundy Cherry Ice Cream. Mix in ¼ cup of the liqueur. Spread half of the mixture in each of two pans; smooth and level the ice cream. Spoon the French Vanilla Ice Cream into the third pan; smooth and level it. Freeze the ice creams. Meanwhile, prepare cake mix according to package directions, using two 8-inch round cake pans. When cake is cool, split each layer horizontally into 4 thin layers. Brush about 2 tablespoons of the remaining liqueur on each layer. Chill cake layers in freezer. To assemble torte, place one layer of cake, cut side up, on a cake plate. Remove one round layer of Burgundy Cherry Ice Cream from the pan; stack on top of first cake layer. Add second cake layer and top with the Vanilla Ice Cream round. If desired, sprinkle with nuts. Add another cake layer, followed by the remaining Burgundy Cherry layer. Place last cake layer, cut side down, firmly on top. Freeze at least 3 hours. Frost the top sides of the torte with the whipped cream; garnish with chocolate curls and cherries. Freeze until served. At serving time, allow the torte to mellow 10 minutes in the refrigerator before cutting into wedges. Makes 10 to 16 servings.

Laurie Schwede, Boulder, Colorado (1975)

CHERRY CHEESE SESAME SUNDAE

Devotees of fruit and cheese for dessert will delight in this sophisticated elaboration.

2 tablespoons sesame seeds	4 tablespoons light cream
1 pint Baskin-Robbins Burgundy Cherry Ice Cream	1 package (3 ounces) cream cheese

Measure sesame seeds into small skillet over medium heat; shake pan until seeds become a light golden brown. Cool. Place cream cheese in a small bowl to soften. Add cream; mix until smooth and stir in one tablespoon of the toasted sesame seeds. Scoop ice cream into 4 individual sherbet or dessert dishes. Top with cream cheese mixture, sprinkle with remaining seeds. Makes 4 servings.

Elizabeth Draper, Austin, Texas (1973)

Baddy Baddy Gumdrop

One of the most promising Baskin-Robbins flavors of the mid-'60's was something called Goody Goody Gumdrop. It embodied everything that is different about Baskin-Robbins—it was unique, used a tasty ingredient people already loved, and above all else was fun. Anticipation was rife as the flavor came squishing out of production and was delivered to the stores. Kids loved its taste, but parents discovered something nobody at Baskin-Robbins had stopped to consider: frozen gumdrops are like so many pebbles in the mouth, and rocks have a tendency to wreak havoc on teeth, children's or adults'. Somehow the flavor was sneaked away. Baskin-Robbins just seems to have been born under the right star.

Mardi Gras

Make a Merry Mardi Gras with these!

MARDI GRAS ICE CREAM PIE
WITH PRALINE SAUCE

2 tablespoons soft butter
1 can (3½ ounces) flaked
   coconut
1 quart Baskin-Robbins
   Butter Pecan Ice
   Cream
1 quart Baskin-Robbins
   Coconut Chocolate
   Chip Ice Cream (or
   Coconut Almond
   Fudge)

1 cup buttermilk
1 tablespoon molasses
½ cup butter
3 tablespoons white corn
   syrup
1 teaspoon baking soda
1 teaspoon vanilla
½ cup coarsely chopped
   pecans, or more
2 cups sugar

Spread the 2 tablespoons of butter in a 9-inch pie
pan; press the coconut into the butter. Bake in a
300-degree oven until a light brown, about 20
minutes. (If edges brown too quickly, cover with
foil and continue baking until done.) Cool shell.
Soften the Butter Pecan Ice Cream and press into
bottom of shell. Freeze for 1 hour. Scoop Nutty
Coconut Ice Cream over the Butter Pecan Ice
Cream. Freeze at least 3 hours. Meanwhile, combine the remaining ingredients, except the vanilla
and pecans, in a heavy saucepan. Bring to a gentle
boil, simmer for 10 minutes, stirring occasionally;
remove from heat. Stir in vanilla and pecans.

(Sauce thickens as it cools.) To serve, cut pie into wedges, pass the Praline Sauce. Makes 8 servings.

Mrs. Lee R. Connell, Jr., New Orleans, Louisiana (1975)

BANANAS MARTINIQUE

Reminiscent of New Orleans' Bananas Foster, this combination of orange, apricot, rum, and banana flavors over ice cream is super.

1 quart Baskin-Robbins French Vanilla Ice Cream	½ cup apricot jam
	1 cup rum
	6 ripe bananas
3 tablespoons butter	¼ cup toasted, sliced almonds
¼ cup sugar	
¾ cup orange juice	

Make 6 large scoops of ice cream. Place in freezer until serving time. In a large chafing dish or skillet, melt butter over medium heat; stir in sugar. Cook, stirring, until sugar caramelizes. Mix in orange juice and apricot jam; heat, stirring constantly, until caramelized sugar is dissolved; stir in rum. Peel banana, slice lengthwise, lay in the hot sauce. Bring just to the simmering point; cook 1 or 2 minutes, turning bananas once. Do not overcook. (If desired, flame with rum.) Place two banana halves on each dessert plate. Top with a scoop of ice cream, a generous spoonful of sauce, and a sprinkle of toasted almonds. Makes 6 servings.

Irene Friday, Osprey, Florida (1973)

Rock 'n Roll Ripple

Baskin-Robbins tries not to be outdone, and sometimes this takes a bit of ingenuity. Not being too up on the rock music scene back in the '60's, Baskin and Robbins didn't know the word "Beatle" from the word "beetle" when a reporter from the Washington *Post* called prior to the group's first U.S. tour in 1964. The reporter assumed Baskin-Robbins would be coming out with a new flavor in the Beatles' honor, and what would it be called? Robbins, caught on the phone and on the hot seat, gulped, then said, "Uh . . . Beatlenut." That was Thursday, and the tour began the following Tuesday. "Somehow," Robbins says now, "we got that flavor made, and it was a good one, had sesame seeds in it, as I recall. We had signs designed and reproduced, and everything, including the ice cream, was in the stores by Monday night. I don't think it would be possible now; there are just too many stores. But you can bet we'd give it a go if we thought it meant something as big as the Beatles."

MARCH

March brings hope. In climates with a long, hard, real-life winter, March almost invariably brings a day when the smell of damp soil and the song of spring birds are in the air. March is the month of spring fever, when jackets replace heavy coats and then heavy coats once again replace jackets. In the more temperate climates March brings an incredible burst of new growth: tender, fragile leaves begin appearing on vegetation of all sorts, blossoms spread, and early-bird gardeners begin tilling their vegetable patches. Although by now you've been indoctrinated well enough to know that ice cream is something to be eaten all year long, perhaps March will bring the first mild day when you feel compelled to buy an ice cream cone and walk along the street eating it. This writer recalls a little bakery store in Oberlin, Ohio, which made a fortune selling greasy donuts and other food to college students at inflated prices. They also featured a flavor or two of mediocre ice cream, which they skimped onto waffle cones for fifteen cents a scoop. Bad as it was, it was virtually the only place in town, and come that first March spring day the campus would swarm with cone-licking students seeking to force the season. But March was fickle back in the Midwest: very often the next day would bring driving sleet, raw winds, and snow once again. One could probably tell just what the weather had been at that time of year by studying that store's sales charts.

The first actual day of spring occurs in March, as does the fabled Ides of March—the day Julius Caesar had been cautioned against, and the day he ultimately was assassinated. Our March calendar includes a salute to, of all things, nuts, and a little bit about a few different kinds. March is National Peanut Month, although we do not necessarily advocate the use of peanuts over other varieties of nuts. After all, what would ice cream be without almonds, walnuts, pecans, and pistachios? You'll find a nice variety of delicious recipes utilizing nuts and nut ice creams—*fan*-tastic!

Should you decide to celebrate the first day of spring in spite of the fickle weather, we have provided you with three special desserts to get you in the mood. Springtime, we're coming!

GOOEY PISCES MELBA

March-born Pisceans, with their propensity toward addictions of all kinds, plus their tendency to overindulge, will love this hodgepodge of flavors. It is a veritable plethora of ingredients. Try it, or better yet, try it out on one of your Pisces friends.

1 package (18.5 ounces) chocolate fudge cake
1 9-inch deep-dish pie shell, baked (unbaked frozen, or home-made)
1 quart Baskin-Robbins Banana Marshmallow Ice Cream
1 teaspoon vanilla
2 tablespoons Grand Marnier or brandy
1 can (16 ounces) Elberta peach slices, drained
3 egg whites
⅓ cup sugar
1 package (10 ounces) frozen raspberries

Bake cake according to package directions in two 9-inch cake pans. When cake layers and pie shell are cool, put one layer of cake in pie shell. (Cut to fit, if necessary.) Wrap in foil; freeze at least 2 hours. (Use other layer in any way desired.) Slightly soften ice cream and smooth into a 9-inch pie pan. Freeze at least 3 hours. The day of serving, thaw raspberries and blend with Grand Marnier. (If desired, thicken raspberries with 2 teaspoons cornstarch; cook over medium heat until slightly thickened, cool, then stir in Grand Marnier.) Make a meringue by beating egg whites until they form soft peaks, gradually beat in sugar, finally blend in vanilla. Assemble dessert by unmolding ice cream with meringue; layer on top of cake, top with well-drained peach slices. Cover ice cream with meringue, sealing meringue to pie shell. Freeze 2 hours. To serve, bake in a preheated 400-degree oven until meringue is a light brown, about 3 minutes. Serve with cold raspberry sauce. Makes 8 to 10 servings.

Marjorie Johnston, St. Louis, Missouri (1975)

Nuts

Next to chocolate and fruits, there's one thing ice cream could never do without: nuts. And Baskin-Robbins has made better use of a wider variety of nuts than anybody in the ice cream business. We've had everything from Butter Pecan to Baseball Nut to Pistachio Almond. Nuts are actually defined as a fruit, or any seed or fruit consisting of a kernel, usually oily, and surrounded by a brittle shell. Nuts are a highly concentrated food, high in fat and protein, and generally very tasty, which quality, combined with their crunchy texture, makes them an ideal ingredient for ice cream. There are well over a hundred different kinds of nuts, although many aren't edible (except possibly by Euell Gibbons).

While coconut actually contains the word *nut*, many people never stopped to think that it really *is* a nut, primarily because of its size and the fact that it is often seen only in shredded form. The Chinese water chestnut, however, is not actually a nut, but a tuber. Cashew nuts, one of the most elegant, fattening, and perhaps expensive of all cocktail nuts, are grown primarily in India and are directly related to poison ivy and poison sumac. All portions of the raw cashew will cause a blistering effect on the skin prior to the nuts' being roasted. Cashew lovers have no fear, though: the roasting dispels any poisonous properties. The United States consumes over seventy percent of the cashew production of India. What else would you expect of the snack capital of the world?

In spite of the fact that some people pay exorbitant prices to get mixed nuts *without* peanuts, the latter is the most popular nut in the U.S. Peanuts are consumed by the millions with drinks, in desserts and candy bars, in ice cream, and in the form of peanut butter. A few years ago Baskin-Robbins came out with several peanut butter/chocolate flavor combinations of ice cream, each one of which was better than the last.

Peanut butter happened to celebrate its eighty-fifth birthday in 1975, by the end of which more than 650 million pounds of the stuff will have been consumed by Americans (just for the one year). That makes it almost as popular as ice cream, but not quite. Interestingly enough, peanut butter has undergone a quality revival similar to that of ice cream. When it was first developed, peanut butter was nothing more than ground-up peanuts with a little salt added. Then, during the age of homogenization, stabilization, and standardization, peanut butter got filled with all kinds of junk and lost a great deal of its character. Now, as with ice cream, genuine peanut butter freaks are demanding the best, nonhydrogenated, nonstabilized stuff.

The peanut itself is a legume and has peas and beans as close relatives. It grows on a vine (average height, around 18 inches) which shoots pegs into the ground. It is from these pegs that the peanuts grow, underneath the soil's surface.

Peanuts originated in South America and were considered edible as early as 750 B.C. Authorities agree that sixteenth-century Spanish and Portuguese colonists introduced peanut growing to Africa and Asia, and it was from Africa that the "goobers" made their way to North America in the seventeenth century. It's been uphill ever since.

Since March is National Peanut Month, according to the people from McLean, Virginia, we have given you a variety of recipes using not only peanuts but many other kinds of nuts in some concoctions that'll make any nut lover's chops drool.

CHOCO-PEANUT BANANA ICE CREAM

¼ cup butter
¼ cup sugar
1 tablespoon flour
1 cup finely chopped
   salted peanuts
2 cups chocolate chips
1 cup whipping or heavy
   cream

1 teaspoon vanilla
1 quart Baskin-Robbins
   Banana Marshmallow
   Ice Cream
2 tablespoons milk
½ cup salted peanuts

To make peanut crust: thoroughly blend butter, sugar, flour, and chopped peanuts. Press into bottom and sides (not rim) of lightly buttered 9-inch pie plate. (To help hold the crust in shape, place an 8-inch pie pan on top of crust.) Bake 8 minutes in a 350-degree oven. If needed, reshape crust. Cool. Chill. In small saucepan, over low heat, melt chocolate chips in whipping cream. Remove from heat; stir in vanilla. Cool. Chill. Spoon slightly softened ice cream into chilled crust. Lightly pour about ⅔ cup of the chocolate sauce over ice cream to produce a marbled effect. Cover with foil. Freeze at least 3 hours. Thin remaining chocolate sauce with enough milk to allow it to pour slowly from spoon. To serve, cut pie into wedges, spoon chocolate sauce over each wedge, and sprinkle with salted peanuts. Makes 6 to 8 servings.

Pamela Schrank, Madison, Wisconsin (1975)

DATE WALNUT TORTE

4 egg whites
6 tablespoons sugar
4 tablespoons brown
   sugar, sifted
1 teaspoon vanilla
½ teaspoon cinnamon
2½ cups finely chopped
   walnuts

1 quart Baskin-Robbins
   Banana Marshmal-
   low Ice Cream
1 recipe Walnut Date
   Sauce (recipe be-
   low)

Line two 9-inch cake pans with brown paper. Make nut-meringue layers by stiffly beating egg whites while slowly adding sugar. Fold in the brown sugar, vanilla, and cinnamon, then stir in walnuts. Evenly divide the meringue mixture between the two pans. Bake in a 350-degree oven for about 25 minutes. Remove from oven; cool in pan. When thoroughly cool, remove meringues from pans. Slightly soften the ice cream; smooth half of the ice cream on each meringue. Stack the two layers into a 4-layer torte. Freeze until firm, about 3 hours. Meanwhile, make walnut date sauce. To serve, garnish top of torte with part of sauce. Cut in wedges; pass sauce. Makes 8 to 12 servings.

Walnut Date Sauce

Marinate 1 cup of coarsely chopped dates in ¼ cup rum for 1 hour. Combine ¼ cup honey, ¼ cup sugar, and ½ cup water. Boil mixture for 5 minutes; cool. Stir cooled syrup into dates and rum. Just before serving, stir in ⅓ cup chopped walnuts.

Maria K. Junge, Los Gatos, California (1975)

So Who Ordered Black Walnut in the First Place?

Over the years, Baskin-Robbins has been hounded by people from every corner of the globe to make Black Walnut ice cream. There have been letters, suggestions to store owners, phone calls, even people banging on the sides of Baskin-Robbins trucks to suggest Black Walnut.

"We finally relented," Irv says, "and during the first two months that flavor was in, we hardly sold a scoop. There are certain flavors people *think* they're going to eat, but when it comes down to it, nobody really does. We get suggestions from people all the time for more Pistachio flavors, but how regularly does anybody eat Pistachio Ice Cream? Same goes with a flavor that seems to be popular in New England, called Frozen Pudding—it's got a rum base and is very similar to our Rum Raisin, but both those flavors are seasonal at best."

NUTTY CHOCOLATE BAR PARFAIT

¼ cup chunky peanut butter
2 tablespoons marshmallow creme
¼ cup hot water
1 pint Baskin-Robbins French Vanilla Ice Cream

2 (1.05 ounces) milk chocolate bars, finely chopped
Whipped cream or topping
2 tablespoons chopped salted peanuts

In small skillet, gently heat peanut butter, marshmallow creme, and hot water, stirring, just until blended. Working quickly, place a scoop of ice cream in the bottom of each of 2 parfait or stemmed water glasses. Spoon ⅓ of the peanut butter sauce evenly over the two scoops of ice cream; sprinkle with ⅓ of the chopped chocolate. Repeat with two more layers. Top with whipped cream and sprinkle with chopped peanuts. Makes 2 generous servings.

John J. Quinn, III, Berkeley, California (1973)

FROZEN VIENNESE TORTE

1 cup apricot jam
⅓ cup brandy
24 lady fingers, split
1 quart Baskin-Robbins Chocolate Almond Ice Cream
1½ cups whipping cream

¾ teaspoon vanilla
3 tablespoons sugar
1 jar (9 ounces) Baskin-Robbins Chocolate Syrup
½ cup toasted sliced almonds

82

Heat jam just until it melts; cool and stir in brandy. Spread 24 lady finger halves with this mixture; top with remaining halves. Lay 12 filled fingers, in a wheel pattern, in bottom of a 9-inch spring-form pan. Slightly soften ice cream, press in, around, and over the filled fingers. Arrange remaining 12 filled fingers, in a wheel pattern, on top of ice cream. Freeze for at least 30 minutes. Meanwhile, beat cream and vanilla until frothy; gradually add sugar and continue beating until stiff. Cover filled fingers with two-thirds of the whipped cream. Cover spring-form pan with foil. Freeze at least 4 hours. Refrigerate remaining cream and plate on which torte will be served. Turn spring-form pan upside down onto chilled plate (whipped cream layer will be on bottom). Drizzle top with some of the chocolate syrup and sprinkle with almonds. Top with a mound of remaining whipped cream. Serve now, or freeze until serving time. If frozen, mellow in refrigerator 15 minutes before cutting into wedges. Makes 8 to 10 servings.

APPLE BUTTER PECAN TARTS

1 pint Baskin-Robbins
    Butter Pecan Ice
    Cream
1 can (16 ounces) ap-
    plesauce
½ cup light brown sugar
½ teaspoon *each* nutmeg
    and cinnamon

¼ teaspoon allspice
5 baked pie-crust tart
    shells (4″ diameter)
3 egg whites
¼ teaspoon cream of tartar
⅓ cup packed dark brown
    sugar
½ teaspoon vanilla

Make 5 scoops of ice cream; put on tray and freeze until firm. Combine applesauce, sugar, and spices in a small saucepan. Cook over low heat, stirring occasionally until mixture is medium thick. Cool; chill. Spoon applesauce mixture into tart shells. Center a scoop of ice cream in each shell. Place in freezer. Beat egg whites and cream of tartar until soft peaks form. Gradually add brown sugar and vanilla, beating until stiff peaks form and mixture is glossy. Remove tarts from freezer; completely cover ice cream with meringue, spreading it to cover edge of shells. (Freeze, at this point, for no longer than 24 hours.) Bake in a preheated 450-degree oven for 2 or 3 minutes, or until meringue is a light golden brown. Makes 5 servings.

BANANA PIES

A sweet little miracle of hot fudge sauce, crunchy peanut butter, and Jamoca® Ice Cream in little banana pies.

½ cup chunky peanut butter

1 jar (9 ounces) Baskin-Robbins Hot Fudge

4 graham cracker shells (4 inch)

2 ripe bananas, peeled

1 pint Baskin-Robbins Jamoca® or Jamoca® Almond Fudge Ice Cream

¼ cup chopped peanuts

Mix peanut butter and hot fudge in a small skillet. Cook, stirring, over low heat just until warmed through. Remove from heat; spoon a tablespoon of sauce into each shell. Slice a half banana into each pie; top each with a large scoop of ice cream. Freeze for 30 minutes or more. If desired, remove from foil pans. To serve: heat remaining sauce and pour over ice cream; sprinkle with peanuts. Makes 4 servings.

Don't Neglect Pistachios

We just couldn't resist adding a little section about pistachios. Pistachio ice cream is one of those flavors that people think they want to eat, but seldom actually buy. Baskin-Robbins has done something to make it more popular, though, by adding other ingredients (such as almonds). Pistachio nuts frighten the unindoctrinated; by the same token, they tend to addict the indoctrinated (this writer is a hopeless pistachio nut, and has developed a rare talent for opening the shells and eating them with tremendous speed). Pistachios by themselves are a healthy food; they are recommended on several special weight-loss diets because they are extremely low in carbohydrates and high in food value. Above all else, they are delicious and, beyond that, they are obnoxiously expensive. A word to the pistachio-wise: if you really crave big, scrumptious pistachios whose shells you don't have to break open with a hammer, try your yellow pages for a local nut distributor or wholesaler.

Pistachios have not been given their just deserts in this country. The pistachio, a member of the cashew family, grows only in dry, warm climates. The pistachios we buy and eat are almost all imported. They are widely cultivated in an area stretching from Afghanistan through the Mediterranean region and have been tried with limited success in California (what hasn't?). The nuts grow in clusters on a broad-branched, deciduous tree which ranges in height from twenty to thirty feet. Contrary to popular American opinion, they do not grow in red and tan varieties, but are exclusively white in their natural state. The green meat of the pistachio fruit has been used for centuries as a dye and food coloring.

PISTACHIO GRASSHOPPER TARTS

2 cups fine chocolate wafer crumbs
½ cup butter or margarine, melted
4 tablespoons confectioners' sugar
¾ cup whipping cream
2 tablespoons sugar
1½ tablespoons white creme de cacao
1½ tablespoons white creme de menthe
1 pint Baskin-Robbins Pistachio Almond Fudge Ice Cream
6 tablespoons chopped pistachio nuts

Blend wafer crumbs with butter and confectioners' sugar. Press into bottoms and sides of five 4-inch tart pans. Bake in a 300-degree oven for 15 minutes. Cool. Freeze. Whip cream, fold in sugar, creme de cacao, and creme de menthe, blending well. Chill. Put one scoop of ice cream in each shell, gently smoothing and leveling ice cream. Carefully remove shells from pans and place on tray. Top and cover each scoop with a generous swirl of the whipped cream mixture. Sprinkle with chopped pistachios. Serve immediately or freeze until needed. Makes 5 servings.

Dorothy Burridge, Tustin, California (1973)

St. Patrick's Day

Don't just wear green on St. Patrick's Day this year; *think* green, and you can even eat a new kind of green with these two recipes. One's a true ice cream spectacular; the other, a super variation on the Grasshopper, a drink that undeservedly has become associated solely with old ladies. If the old ladies are drinking this at their whist parties, they must be having a better time than we thought!

ST. PATRICK'S PINEAPPLE SUPREME

1 can (20 ounces) crushed pineapple
¼ cup green creme de menthe
2 quarts Baskin-Robbins French Vanilla Ice Cream
1 pint Baskin-Robbins Lemon Custard Ice Cream
1 quart Baskin-Robbins Chocolate Almond Ice Cream
1 pint heavy cream, whipped
Green food coloring, optional
¼ cup toasted sliced almonds

Thoroughly drain pineapple and mix with creme de menthe; let stand at least 2 hours. Thoroughly chill an 8-inch, two-quart bundt pan. Firmly press the vanilla ice cream into the chilled pan, making a 1½-inch lining on the bottom and sides of the pan. (The lining will not reach the top of the pan; be sure that the sides are level.) Freeze until firm. Thoroughly drain the crushed pineapple; reserve the creme de

menthe. Soften the Lemon Custard Ice Cream; fold in one-half of the drained pineapple. Spoon this mixture into the cavity of the vanilla ice cream-lined pan. Level; freeze until firm, about 3 hours. Spoon slightly softened Chocolate Almond Ice Cream into cavity, filling to top of pan. Freeze until firm. Whip cream until stiff; fold in 2 tablespoons of reserved creme de menthe. If desired, add a few drops of green food coloring. Remove pan from freezer; dip briefly in lukewarm water. Place a serving plate on top; invert and gently tap pan to unmold. (If surface is melted, return to freezer until firm. Put the tinted whipped cream into a pastry bag and flute along the lines of the molded ice cream. Sprinkle with almonds. Freeze until serving time. (If desired, pass remaining pineapple and creme de menthe, combined, as a sauce.) Makes 20 servings.

Teresa A. Satow, Parma, Ohio (1975)

FROSTY GRASSHOPPER

1 pint Baskin-Robbins
Pistachio Almond
Ice Cream
2½ tablespoons green
creme de menthe

2 tablespoons creme de
cacao
Whipped cream or
topping
2 sprigs of mint

Combine creme de cacao, 2 tablespoons of the creme de menthe, and the ice cream in blender; cover, blend just until smooth. Pour into 2 tall glasses. Top with whipped cream. Swirl remaining creme de menthe into cream. Garnish with sprigs of mint. Makes 2 servings.

Dorothy Burridge, Tustin, California (1975)

First Day of Spring

The first day of spring brings two recipes, one simple, one more complicated, both equally delicious.

CASSATA FOR SPRINGTIME

⅔ cup sugar
¼ cup water
3 egg whites
stiffly beaten
½ cup chopped almonds
and pistachio nuts
½ cup diced fresh
strawberries

1 pint whipping or heavy
cream, whipped
1 quart Baskin-Robbins
Fresh Strawberry Ice
Cream
1 quart Baskin-Robbins
Pistachio Almond Ice
Cream

Cook sugar and water until mixture reaches the soft ball stage (236 degrees on a candy thermometer). Add sugar syrup gradually to beaten egg whites while beating; beat until mixture forms stiff peaks. Fold nuts and fruit into meringue. Fold in three-fourths of the whipped cream, blending well. Freeze. Freeze a 3-quart round mold. Soften the Fresh Strawberry Ice Cream just to spreading consistency and line the inside of the frozen mold to a depth of ½ inch. Freeze about 3 hours. Repeat the process with the Pistachio Almond Ice Cream, adding a ½-inch layer of that flavor. Freeze 3 hours. Fill remaining cavity with the frozen meringue filling. Freeze until firm, about 2 hours. To serve, turn out of mold onto serving platter. Garnish with remaining whipped cream, and whole fresh strawberries, if desired. Makes 10 to 12 servings.

Pamela B. Muir, Claremont, California (1975)

HONEYSUCKLE CREAM

Just plain good for sipping as dessert or perk-up drink. In blender or small bowl blend 3 scoops of Baskin-Robbins Lemon Custard Ice Cream, 1 tablespoon honey, ¼ cup rum, and 1 cup milk just until smooth. Pour into 4 small cocktail glasses. Makes 4 servings.

Mary Hrvatin, Spokane, Washington (1973)

This is a moody month when everything changes. One day it seems like summer has come for good, the next it couldn't seem further away. Robert Frost states it pretty well in this excerpt from "Two Tramps in Mud Time":

The sun was warm but the wind was chill.
You know how it is with an April day
When the sun is out and the wind is still,
You're one month on in the middle of May.
But if you so much as dare to speak,
A cloud comes over the sunlit arch,
A wind comes off a frozen peak,
And you're two months back in the middle of
    March.

But April's a great time for ice cream—parties begin to blossom again, and you'll find some super party goodies for all sorts of occasions right here. April first begins National Laugh Week, so join in and wipe off that sour winter expression.

April Fool's Day

April begins with April Fool's Day. The meaning of this day is crystal clear to schoolkids: it's a great time to put frogs down people's (most often teacher's) backs, tell lies legally, and practice all manner of other normally antisocial behavior. But the origins of the tradition are not so clear. The most popular opinion is that since March 25 was formerly New Year's Day, April 1 was its octave, or a full week later, when New Year's festivities formally ended. Somehow that has come to be April Fool's Day. Or it may be a leftover from the Roman Cerealia, held at the beginning of April—the tale was that Proserpina, gamboling in the meadows picking daffodils.

Fool everybody on April Fool's Day by serving these super Peanutty Banana Squares, second prize winners in the 1975 Show Off. They were submitted by Dorothy Burridge of Tustin, California, one of BR's most loyal fans and creative cooks. When the final judging was made, it happened that Mrs. Burridge, a winner in the '73 Show Off, had two recipes in the top categories. Because no one can win more than one prize, one had to be chosen over the other, and these Banana Squares emerged the victor. You will find several more of Mrs. Burridge's recipes throughout this book, however. Thank you, Dorothy Burridge.

PEANUTTY BANANA SQUARES

1½ tablespoons sugar
2 tablespoons banana liqueur, optional
½ cup whipping cream, whipped
⅓ cup chunky peanut butter
¼ cup Baskin-Robbins Hot Fudge

1 pint Baskin-Robbins Banana Marshmallow Ice Cream
1½ cups Baskin-Robbins Chocolate Chip Ice Cream
1 cup crushed peanut brittle

Fold sugar (and liqueur, if used) into whipped cream. Refrigerate. Blend peanut butter and hot fudge. Working quickly, spread Banana Marshmallow Ice Cream, or any other Baskin-Robbins banana-flavored ice cream, evenly in an 8-inch square pan. With knife, mark off 9 squares, 3 across and 3 down. With back of spoon, make an indentation in center of each square. Spoon 1 tablespoon of peanut butter-fudge mixture into each indentation. Sprinkle ½ cup crushed brittle around indentations. Spread Chocolate Chip Ice Cream over all; gently press down to level top. Swirl whipped cream mixture over top; sprinkle with remaining crushed brittle. (Peanut butter-fudge filling will be centered in each square.) Freeze until firm, about 3 hours. To serve, cut into 9 squares. Makes 9 servings.

Dorothy Burridge, Tustin, California (1975)

Aries

Who ever heard of an ice cream taco? If anybody did, it would have to be an Aries. Anything to be different. One Aries friend once recommended Liver and Onions Ice Cream as a new flavor for Baskin-Robbins. Others have thought Pizza Ice Cream would top everything, so these somewhat silly tacos are just perfect for all you defiant Arians.

TACOS TERRIFICOS

1 pint Baskin-Robbins Chocolate Almond Ice Cream	½ teaspoon water
	¾ cup flaked coconut
12 crisp taco shells	1 pint Baskin-Robbins Butter Pecan Ice Cream
3 drops green food coloring	

Press a small scoop of Chocolate Almond Ice Cream in the bottom of each taco shell. Freeze for 30 minutes. In glass jar, dilute food coloring with water; add coconut. Cover. Shake vigorously; set aside. Remove some of the tacos from freezer; add a small scoop of Butter Pecan Ice Cream on top of the Chocolate Almond. Garnish tops with green coconut and return to freezer. Continue until all are finished. Makes 12 servings.

Mary J. Peterson, Arvada, Colorado (1973)

Vermont Maple Festival

The first week in April is a special time in Vermont, where maple reigns supreme. This is the Vermont Maple Festival, celebrating the state's most famous and most unique product. For years, smart New Englanders have been pouring fresh maple syrup over vanilla, coffee, and other flavors of ice cream, but here we have a simple dessert that combines the flavors of bananas and peanuts with pure maple syrup.

BANANA-BRITTLE BITES

1 package (12 ounces)
   peanut brittle
1 quart Baskin-Robbins
   Fresh Banana Ice
   Cream

¼ cup peanut butter
½ cup pure maple syrup

Crush peanut brittle into fine crumbs. Using a tablespoon or melon baller, scoop Fresh Banana Ice Cream, or any other Baskin-Robbins banana-flavored ice cream, into balls the size of a small walnut. Quickly roll each ball in crushed brittle and place in shallow pan in the freezer. Continue until all of the ice cream is used. Freeze 3 to 4 hours. Serve on pretty plates with dessert picks or toothpicks. Pass a sauce of blended peanut butter and syrup. Makes about 30 pieces.

Pauline B. Kauffman, Phoenix, Arizona (1975)

• • •

Press agents and others connected with the film industry are always trying to tie in movie names with new flavor ideas. Sometimes it works, sometimes it doesn't. Remember Peachy Mame, Steverino, Jack Lemmon? A few years ago we had a great suggestion: "The Last Mango in Burbank."

• • •

Volcano Day

Since we received this recipe entitled Lemon Lava Volcanoes, we couldn't resist going to the trusty *Guinness' Book of World Records* (in which Baskin-Robbins was listed, by the way, for having produced the greatest number of ice cream flavors—405 in all) to find some volcano trivia. It happens that the greatest volcanic eruption ever recorded was that of Tambora, a crater on the island of Sumbawa, Indonesia, on April 7, 1815. The volcano lost about 4,100 feet in height and formed a crater seven miles in diameter. The internal pressure of the volcano that fateful April 7 has been estimated at 46,500,000 pounds per square inch. So put that in your Lemon Lava Volcanoes and eat them.

LEMON LAVA VOLCANOES

1 container (4½ ounces)
    frozen non-dairy
    whipped topping,
    thawed
1 quart Baskin-Robbins
    Lemon Custard Ice
    Cream

Green creme de menthe
Lemon slices, optional
Mint sprigs, optional
Green food coloring

Tint whipped topping with green food coloring to a pale green. Using ¼ cup topping for each mound, form 8 mounds, each 3 inches in diameter, on a wax-paper-lined baking sheet. Make a depression in top of each mound with a spoon. Freeze 3 hours. To serve, place shells on individual dessert plates. Fill each depression with a scoop of ice cream. Drizzle with creme de menthe. If desired, garnish with lemon slices and mint sprigs. Makes 8 servings.
Marlene E. Johnson, St. Paul, Minnesota (1975)

Roppongi Magic

Ice cream magic begets ice cream magic, no matter where in the world you go. Shortly after the first Baskin-Robbins store opened in Tokyo in April, 1974, a land owner named Hitoshi Kikuchi discovered the ice cream, and it soon became his passion. He owned a house on a large, valuable, and picturesque parcel of land situated in the heart of the now-booming Roppongi area of Tokyo. Plans had been made to erect yet another skyscraper office building on this parcel, which had been planted over the years with trees and flowering foliage of every possible description. Realizing that what the overly commercial area needed was a park or public area, and certainly not another office building, Hitoshi instigated a plan to raze the house but leave the beautiful gardens, as a pleasant place for people to enjoy. When his lawyers advised him this would be financially unfeasible, Hitoshi approached Baskin-Robbins Japan, and a plan was devised to enhance the park with the magic of a Baskin-Robbins store, combined with a small florist's shop. Now people could not only see and smell the beautiful flowers in the park; they could take them home and enjoy an ice cream treat as well! The Roppongi Baskin-Robbins in Torizaka Garden will undoubtedly always remain the most magical, beautifully situated ice cream shop in the world.

101

Baskin-Robbins' international locations in 1975 staged their own recipe contests. The grand prize winner from Belgium is featured during the month of December, commemorating the opening date of the first Belgian store. Following is the unique and attractive Bridal Hat, submitted by Mrs. H. Seto of Tokyo and awarded grand prize for Japanese entries.

BRIDAL HAT

1 pint Baskin-Robbins
    Vanilla Ice Cream
1 pint Baskin-Robbins
    Fresh Strawberry
    Ice Cream
1 pint Baskin-Robbins
    Burgundy Cherry
    Ice Cream

1 pint Baskin-Robbins
    Pistachio Almond
    Fudge Ice Cream
Lady fingers and whipped
    cream

Place the ice creams in two 9-inch cake tins in layers. Level top. Freeze until firm. Remove from tins. Stack one on top of the other. Place on a serving plate. Press lady fingers around the sides of the cake. Wrap a bright red ribbon around the cake; tie in a bow. Cover top with whipped cream. Return to freezer at least one hour.

Mrs. H. Seto, Tokyo, Japan (1975)

Easter Sunday

Whether you're celebrating Easter or just the arrival of springtime, this light sherbet-ice cream dessert will help you out. Be inventive and substitute other combinations of ice cream and sherbet to fill the cream puffs.

BING CHERRY PEACH PARFAIT PUFF

½ cup water
½ cup shortening or margarine
⅛ teaspoon salt
½ cup all-purpose flour
2 eggs
2 large ripe peaches (optional)

1 quart Baskin-Robbins Chilled Bing Cherry Sherbet
1 quart Baskin-Robbins Fresh Peach Ice Cream

Heat oven to 400 degrees. In a saucepan bring water and shortening to a rolling boil. Stir in, all at once, the flour and salt. Stir vigorously over low heat until the mixture will pull easily from the side of the pan and form a ball (about one minute). Remove from heat. Cool slightly. Stir in eggs; beat mixture until smooth and velvety. Spread in the bottom of a greased 9-inch heat-resistant pie pan. Do not spread on the sides. Bake in a preheated 400-degree oven for 50 minutes, until golden. Remove from pan and place on a rack. Allow to cool slowly, away from drafts. To serve, place alternating slices of Baskin-Robbins Chilled Bing Cherry Sherbet and

103

Fresh Peach Ice Cream into the shell. Cut in wedges; serve at once. (Or, to make this a true do-ahead put filled shell in freezer. Ten minutes before serving remove from freezer and put in refrigerator for 5 to 10 minutes to mellow before cutting into wedges.) If desired, top with a layer of sliced, sweetened fresh peaches. Makes 8 to 10 servings.

When April pulls one of its surprises and turns cold and wet, try this rich, hot coffee variation.

COFFEE-MOCHA-RUM

1 egg yolk	½ teaspoon vanilla
¼ cup powdered sugar	Hot, strong coffee
¼ cup cocoa	1 quart Baskin-Robbins
3 tablespoons dark rum	Chocolate Fudge or
½ cup whipping or heavy	French Vanilla Ice
cream	Cream

Ahead of time, sift sugar and cocoa into egg, add rum, and beat until fluffy. Whip cream with vanilla until soft-stiff peaks form. Fold egg mixture into whipped cream. Refrigerate. Just before serving, brew strong coffee in the amount needed for individual servings. Pour hot coffee into individual cups and add one scoop of ice cream. Immediately spoon 2 tablespoons of rum sauce over each scoop of ice cream. Makes about 8 servings.

Vicky Merrick, Oakland, California (1975)

So You Want to Have a Recipe Contest?

As we mentioned in the introduction, a great many of the fantastic recipes included in this book have come from loyal Baskin-Robbins fans through two Ice Cream Show Off recipe contests, staged in 1973 and 1975. The contests are like any other national recipe competition, only maybe a little bit more fun because the main ingredient is ice cream. The contest was developed through Baskin-Robbins' public relations department in association with Baskin-Robbins' well-known home economist, Corris Guy, and her associate, Marjorie Nyrop. Working with Baskin-Robbins' energetic Public Relations Manager Marilyn Novak, these two highly qualified professionals planned an event to rival the greatest, most well established recipe contests in the United States.

The logistics of planning such a contest are somewhat overwhelming: setting down guidelines, mapping out categories, planning the promotion and advertising, obtaining prizes, setting up merchandising—all these things take a great deal of time and must occur so far in advance of the actual opening of the contest one tends to lose sight of what it was all about in the first place.

But as soon as those entries begin pouring in the

vision returns, and it is a phenomenal experience for those associated with Baskin-Robbins to realize that there are that many truly loyal fans out there. Men and women don't just send in recipes—they send in creations, works of art, a part of themselves. Entries come in with multicolored illustrations, clever sayings and poems—some are even done with caligraphy. People care.

As soon as the entries begin arriving they are separated by category (Baskin-Robbins has four: ice cream for drinks, ice cream for spooning, ice cream for little "do-aheads," and ice cream for spectacular "do-aheads") and apportioned out to one of five professional home economists whose important job it is to pore over each recipe and decide whether or not it merits final consideration. With thousands of entries in each category this is no easy task, particularly since many recipes are similar. But not everyone can be a winner, and the BR home economists must use their excellent judgment in deciding just which recipes qualify to be made up and tasted at the long and involved preliminary judging. If two recipes appear quite similar, the judges make each up, group-taste it, and then decide. As with the preliminary and final judgings, many considerations go into this decision: is the recipe particularly difficult to make? Has the entrant clearly defined the instructions? Does the recipe utilize ice cream in an interesting or unusual manner? Does the recipe combine ingredients in an artful and creative way? And so on . . .

Finally, the recipes are narrowed down to about a hundred—twenty-five in each category—and the preliminary judging begins. Ingredients must be bought, cakes made, sauces concocted, pieces assembled. Each category is given one day when all the home economists, Marilyn, Marjorie, and Corris get together to taste and taste again. Marilyn Novak claims that she has gained nearly ten pounds during the course of each recipe judging, but it never seems to show. Some people have all the luck.

The tasting is fascinating. The novice learns very quickly—and usually the hard way—that no experienced taste-tester takes big bites; little spoonfuls of each entry do quite nicely when you are spending a whole day tasting twenty-five or more delicious creations. Actual judging is all done by secret ballot (score sheet), and totals in each category are tallied at the end of each day. Celery and carrot sticks, savory meat, and even dill pickles serve as refreshing lunch for this group on these sweet, saucy, cold, and creamy "judgment days."

Scores are tallied, added together, and the numbers do all the talking. The top six recipes in each category—twenty-four recipes in all—then qualify to be judged at the final Show Off one week later.

Judges are flown in from all over the country. Among their ranks have been the likes of Willie

Mae Rogers, Director of the Good Housekeeping Institute, and Mary Eckley, Food Editor of *McCall's* magazine.

Judging is a serious business, and ethics are stringently maintained. No one of the five judges is allowed to comment on any given recipe as it is tasted, although a few value judgments generally slip out after the initial tasting when something is particularly outstanding. Coffee and water are sipped between tastings. The day is not without humor, as not everything goes smoothly. This past year, the dessert case containing all the spectacular desserts rebelled the night before the final judging: when Nancy Davis, BR's dessert decorating specialist, looked in on those "beautiful" desserts the morning of the Show Off, all she saw was six plates of soupy ice cream and drippy toppings, melting, in certain cases, over some soggy cake. The temperature of the dessert case had soared to forty above during the night. All was not lost, however, only because of the loyalty and dedication of the BR home economists, who were summoned and somehow managed to remake each of the desserts prior to their final judging that afternoon. Such is the spirit of Baskin-Robbins.

Irv Robbins says people are constantly asking him how he keeps from getting fat; other people are always saying, "Is he a big fat guy?" And Irv just answers all such questions with: "Ice cream isn't fattening—that's a myth. It's only fattening if you eat other things too." Seriously, though, Irv says anyone with a passion for ice cream needn't be overweight at all. In *The New Yorker* a few years ago, Irv mentioned that he eats ice cream many times a day, including some kind of fruit flavor (generally Fresh Banana) on his morning cereal. His simple rule for staying slim is to substitute the ice cream for some equally caloric (and possibly not even so nutritious) food such as bread, potatoes, that extra glass or two of wine, or whatever. The mark of a true ice cream connoisseur.

Paul Revere Day

Just to show there aren't any hard feelings, have a crack at this English Trifle on Paul Revere Day. After all, it has been two hundred years!

ENGLISH TRIFLE

8 lady fingers, split	1 quart Baskin-Robbins Burgundy Cherry Ice Cream
⅓ cup raspberry or strawberry jam	
⅓ cup orange juice	3 tablespoons powdered sugar
3 tablespoons cherry wine	
8 almond or coconut macaroons, crushed	½ teaspoon vanilla
¾ cup whipping cream	½ cup sliced or slivered almonds, toasted

Spread split lady fingers with jam. Arrange in a single layer, jam side up, in the bottom of an 8-inch square pan. Mix orange juice and cherry wine; pour over lady fingers. Sprinkle with crushed macaroons and cover with three-fourths of the ice cream. Freeze at least 3 hours. For individual servings, place lady fingers in bottom of 8 freezer-proof glass dessert or sherbet dishes. Divide ingredients and layer as described above. Freeze until firm. Just before serving, whip cream, powdered sugar, and vanilla. Swirl over ice cream. Sprinkle with toasted almonds. Makes 8 to 9 servings.

Linda E. Nagy, Cleveland, Ohio (1975)

Baseball and BR

You Mets fans will be eating genuine BR Ice Cream at Shea Stadium this season. And for all you other sports fans who are tired of the plain old neopolitan bars they always serve at stadiums and arenas, we're working on it! Think of how great it'll be to watch your favorite game eating Jamoca® Almond Fudge or Pralines 'n Cream!

When Walter O'Malley brought the Dodgers to Los Angeles in 1957, Baskin-Robbins honored L.A.'s good fortune with a new flavor. Baskin said, "Well, the Dodgers are from Brooklyn, so we've got to get a few raspberries in there." Robbins added, "We're a bunch of baseball nuts anyway." So they added some cashew nuts and Baseball Nut—now another popular flavor—was born. Not wanting to be too partial to baseball, BR later created Hold That Lime, and plans to follow it up with a Forward Pass-tachio.

May is the ideal month of spring, and the honest-to-goodness beginning of the traditional ice cream season. But we have been eating ice cream in various ways, shapes, and forms all year long, haven't we? If you're lucky May is the month you take your first swim, get your first sunburn.

The birds' songs seem louder and better in May, because they haven't been around for a while. One May morning when the young leaves are spreading and the daffodils are in bloom—that makes up for all that depressing waiting back in March and April.

May has its Maypole, Mother's Day, junior proms, and the first cook-out. And by Memorial Day it's pretty certain that summer is really on the way again. The sunburns on the passengers in the cars in the bumper-to-bumper holiday-weekend traffic prove that.

Taurus

Taurus' penchant toward self-indulgence is surpassed only by his love of ease. This drink, a hedonist's dream, combines all the attributes of a superduper banana split without the hassle of having to bite or even chew!

TAURUS BANANA SPLIT

2 scoops Baskin-Robbins Fresh Banana Ice Cream
¾ cup cold milk
1 banana, split lengthwise
Whipped cream, optional

1 scoop each Baskin-Robbins Fresh Strawberry, Chocolate, and French Vanilla Ice Cream
Maraschino cherry, optional

Make a milkshake by blending Fresh Banana Ice Cream and milk to a medium consistency. Pour into a tall soda glass. Add 1 scoop each of Fresh Strawberry, Chocolate, and French Vanilla Ice Cream. Put a banana half on each side of glass. If desired, top with a dollop of whipped cream and a cherry. Makes 1 large serving.

Sharon O'Donnell, Atlanta, Georgia (1975)

May Day

Start May off right with ice cream cones like you've never had before. These things are like something out of a candyland dream.

COOKIE CRUMB ICE CREAM CONES

12 2½-inch paper baking cups	1½ cups crushed chocolate cream-filled cookies
6 red or green maraschino cherries, halved	12 scoops Baskin-Robbins Pistachio Almond Ice Cream, softened
¼ cup chopped almonds	12 Baskin-Robbins sugar cones
¾ cup whipped cream	

Place baking cups in large muffin pan tins to keep firm while filling. Place 1 cherry half in center of a baking cup, cut side up. Sprinkle with 1 teaspoon chopped almonds. Spread with 1 tablespoon whipped cream. Sprinkle with 1 tablespoon cookie crumbs. Gently spoon on half-scoop (approximately 3 tablespoons) ice cream, spreading to level; sprinkle with 1 tablespoon cookie crumbs. Spoon on second half-scoop of ice cream. Place a sugar cone over top, pushing down gently into top of ice cream (be sure paper cup is outside, not under, edge of cone.) Follow same procedure for remaining cones. Freeze until needed. Peel paper cups off carefully before serving. Makes 12 cones.

Dorothy Burridge, Tustin, California (1975)

• • •

In recent years Baskin-Robbins plants have produced nearly 60,000 gallons of ice cream per day! That works out to a daily tally of 2,160,000 scoops of ice cream.

• • •

Mocha Month

Try these individual treats after you're tired of dancing around the Maypole. May is Mocha Month!

MAY DAY JAMOCA® TOWERS

1 package (4½ ounces) instant chocolate fudge pudding mix	1 cup chopped pecans
1¾ cups cold milk	1 jar (9¾ ounces) Baskin-Robbins Butterscotch Topping
1 container (4½ ounces) frozen whipped topping, thawed	1 pint Baskin-Robbins Jamoca® Ice Cream

Prepare pudding according to package directions for pie filling, using the 1¾ cups milk. Chill, about ½ hour, until almost set. Fold in whipped topping and ½ cup of the chopped pecans. Drop by ½ cupfuls onto a wax-paper-lined baking sheet. Make a depression in the center of each and build up sides slightly to hold a scoop of ice cream. Freeze the shells until firm, about 3 hours. To serve, heat butterscotch topping until just warm; stir in remaining pecans. Place a scoop of ice cream in each frozen shell. Spoon over warm topping. Makes 6 servings.

Barbara Binkiwitz, Odessa, New York (1975)

BRAZILIAN FUDGE SUNDAE

3 tablespoons butter or margarine	¾ teaspoon cinnamon
1 square (1 ounce) unsweetened chocolate	Dash of salt
2 tablespoons unsweetened cocoa	1 tablespoon grated orange rind, or more
½ cup sugar	⅓ cup slivered almonds
½ cup heavy or whipping cream	1 quart Baskin-Robbins Jamoca® Ice Cream

Melt butter and chocolate in a heavy pan; stir in cocoa, sugar, cream, cinnamon, and salt. Bring to a boil, stirring constantly. Remove from heat; mix in rind and almonds. Serve warm, (not hot) over scoops of Jamoca® Almond Ice Cream. (Great as parfait, too.) Makes 6 to 8 servings.

Evelyn S. Nelson, Chicago, Illinois (1975)

JAMOCA® CRUNCH BANANA PIE

1¾ cups plain natural cereal

2 squares (1 ounce each) semisweet chocolate

1 tablespoon butter

1 large ripe banana, sliced

1 quart Baskin-Robbins Jamoca® Almond Fudge Ice Cream

1 recipe Mocha Cream (recipe below)

Chocolate curls and sliced almonds, optional

Pour cereal into a small greased bowl. In a small saucepan melt chocolate and butter; blend well and pour over cereal; toss lightly to mix. Spread mixture in a deep, greased 1-inch pie pan. Chill. Arrange banana slices on bottom of crust. Spoon slightly softened ice cream into crust, pressing down evenly with back of spoon. Swirl Mocha Cream over pie. Sprinkle with chocolate curls and almonds, if desired. Freeze until firm, about 3 hours. Makes 8 servings.

Mocha Cream

Whip 1 cup whipping or heavy cream, sweetened. Beat in 1 teaspoon instant coffee and 2 tablespoons hot chocolate powder.

Millie Snow, Southfield, Michigan (1975)

Baskin-Robbins three-gallon ice cream tubs can be useful in a variety of ways. Store owners will be happy to save them for you—just ask. The containers make perfect wastebaskets, and are great projects for kids or adults. Cover them with paper, wallpaper, fabrics, pictures cut out of magazines— you name it—and you've got an attractive, free wastebasket. One creative apartment dweller collected about a dozen of the containers, stacked them on their sides, and used them to store a variety of office supplies, magazines, sewing supplies, and other items.

Be Kind to Animals Week

All ice cream lovers are animal lovers too, right? In honor of May's Be Kind to Animals Week we offer . . .

TURTLES ON SUNDAE

1 quart Baskin-Robbins Butter Pecan Ice Cream	1 jar (9 ounces) Baskin-Robbins Hot Fudge, warmed
1 jar (9¾ ounces) Baskin-Robbins Butterscotch Topping	36 pecan halves

Place a large scoop of ice cream in each of 6 shallow dessert dishes. Smooth each with spoon into an oval mound (to form the turtle's body). On each mound arrange a pecan half to form a head, 4 halves for feet, and a broken piece for a tail. Top each mound with butterscotch topping, then with hot fudge. Serve immediately. Makes 6 servings.

Monica L. Cole, Iowa City, Iowa (1975)

Tigers on Monday

Animals have always been great lovers of ice cream—particularly Baskin-Robbins. And Baskin-Robbins staff members, being the wonderful, humanitarian, philanthropic types that they are, are all animal lovers, so one can imagine the number of animals who get to sample ice cream treats gratis. One former editor of the in-house publication was particularly fond of posing various animals in cute situations eating ice cream, and she came across with some real winners. Having noticed a woman one day in front of the Baskin-Robbins headquarters store feeding ice cream to her full-grown tiger and his poodle companion, this enterprising editor arranged a photo session.

On the morning of the shooting, personnel seemed to crawl out of the woodwork to watch this hefty tiger slink about behind the ice cream counter to have his picture taken. Although his trainer had assured everyone her charge was perfectly harmless, most wise onlookers kept back a few steps (outside the store). The tiger performed beautifully, sitting, standing, climbing on the back bar, but mostly enjoying about four gallons of his favorite, French Vanilla.

We hear other stories, such as the one about the parakeet that repeats incessantly, "Jamoca® Almond Fudge, Jamoca® Almond Fudge," . . . or the dog who fetches his leash and goes to his master and begs when he wants to be taken to Baskin-Robbins (the dog just gets the leash, but doesn't sit up and beg when he wants to be taken out for other reasons). The most unusual animal story was that of a woman whose Siamese cat would normally jump at the chance to devour any Baskin-Robbins flavor; when the cat is pregnant, however (which seems to be rather often), she will touch nothing but Strawberry. The store owner tells of the day the woman came in with the cat, ordered a cone with a scoop each of Chocolate and Jamoca®, and offered the cat a bit of each on a napkin. When the cat daintily turned up her nose, the woman exclaimed, "Oh God, not again!"

Celebrity Facts

If Baskin-Robbins has become known for any one thing, it is certainly for its great number and variety of ice cream flavors. Johnny Carson one night quipped that his home town was so small the Baskin-Robbins store only had two flavors.

• • •

Jack Benny's favorite flavor was Pistachio, since he loved anything that was green. Several years ago Frank Sinatra had planned a birthday party for the late Mr. Benny in Palm Springs. Irv Robbins heard about it and sent Benny thirty-nine quarts of ice cream. Benny's letter, by return mail, stated, "Dear Mr. Robbins, if you're giving away ice cream, I'd like you to be among the first to learn that this was my 78th, not my 39th birthday."

• • •

Totie Fields once said, "I get Baskin-Robbins attacks. I've eaten all of their 31 flavors—sometimes in one day."

• • •

Dear Abby is also a big Baskin-Robbins fan; in fact, during one trip to Los Angeles she commissioned a bellhop to go from her hotel to the Beverly Hills Baskin-Robbins store for a quart of Pralines 'n Cream. Says Abby, "If I don't have my daily Baskin-Robbins fix, I get withdrawal symptoms." In a letter to Irv Robbins, Abby said, "I have no suggestions for a new flavor. But I do have a suggestion for you, Irv. Please don't ever take Pralines 'n Cream off the market. It's worth every calorie, and I not only *can*, but *do* consume a quart in one sitting. Sign me, 'Hooked in Beverly Hills.'"

Abby was in good company with her request for Pralines 'n Cream. Baskin-Robbins has received actual petitions with as many as a hundred signatures demanding that Pralines 'n Cream be added as a regular flavor twelve months out of the year. In Santa Barbara, California, a group of university students picketed their local store until the weary store owner called Burbank and pleaded for a special order of the flavor.

• • •

One thing ought to be made clear: scheduling flavors is not as easy task. Everybody's favorite is not the same, certainly, but even ice cream freaks have to realize that patience is a virtue, and eventually their favorite will return. Among the considerations in scheduling are balancing sherbets and ices with ice creams, plugging in certain flavors for specific holidays, watching out for too many chocolates all at once, too many flavors of the same color, and so on. Some flavors can only be available at certain times because they utilize fresh ingredients whose availability is limited. Such is the plight of the flavor scheduler.

Anyway, Pralines 'n Cream will be around for a while—maybe not forever—but certainly for quite a while. After all, we can't disappoint Dear Abby.

Mother's Day

Desperately trying not to appear sexist in either direction, we have provided two recipes for use on Mother's Day which are both delicious and not too difficult to make. This does not assume that no one but Mother knows how to make anything difficult—just let it rest that on a beautiful spring Sunday who wants to spend time messing around the kitchen? Enough said.

LOVIN' CREAM LEMON PARFAIT

⅓ cup (½ of 6-ounce can) frozen lemonade concentrate
1 cup dairy sour cream
1 pint Baskin-Robbins Lemon Custard Ice Cream

1 pint Baskin-Robbins Fresh Coconut Ice Cream
½ cup toasted flaked coconut

Mix lemonade concentrate and sour cream. Place 1 scoop of Lemon Custard Ice Cream in each of 6 chilled parfait glasses. Top with 1 tablespoon of the lemonade-sour cream mixture. Add a scoop of Fresh Coconut Ice Cream; top with a tablespoon of the lemonade-sour cream mixture. Continue to alternate these layers until glass is filled. Top filled glasses with toasted coconut. Makes 8 to 10 servings.

Mrs. Harry R. Hofford, Phoenix, Arizona (1975)

MOM'S SUNDAES

If your weakness is orange carmel candy, this is your sauce and your dish of ice cream. Quick, crunchy, and velvety-rich.

½ cup crushed peanut brittle	½ cup sugar
1 quart Baskin-Robbins Butter Pecan Ice Cream	½ cup packed brown sugar
	½ cup orange juice

Mix sugars and orange juice in small saucepan. Bring to a boil; cook over low heat, stirring occasionally, for 10 minutes, or until mixture is quite thick. Cool. Place 2 scoops of ice cream in each of 4 sherbet dishes. Spoon sauce over ice cream; sprinkle with peanut brittle. Makes 4 servings.

Mrs. Helen M. Godwin, Greensboro, North Carolina (1973)

KENTUCKY DERBY DAY SUNDAE

Whether or not you're into horses or racing, this sauce is a Colonel's masterpiece, worthy of everyone's attention. Don't hesitate; run to the blender and mix it!

2 ounces unsweetened chocolate
¼ cup sugar
¼ cup light corn syrup
⅛ teaspoon salt
3 tablespoons Kentucky bourbon
⅓ cup hot milk
1 quart Baskin-Robbins Chocolate Mint Ice Cream

Cut chocolate in pieces; put chocolate with next 4 ingredients in blender. Add hot milk; blend until smooth. Cool. Into 4 parfait glasses, alternate layers of sauce and ice cream, ending with sauce. Serve at once or place in freezer. If frozen, allow to mellow in refrigerator for 10 minutes before serving. Makes 4 servings.

Phillip H. Harris, Lexington, Kentucky (1973)

• • •

Speaking of horses, J. Paul Getty's daughter has 31 horses, each named after a Baskin-Robbins flavor.

• • •

Ice Cream Pool

Who in the world would be the first to have a swimming pool shaped like an ice cream cone? If

126

Liberace can have one shaped like a piano, then Irv Robbins can certainly have a cone. And he does, at his home in Encino, and the pool just happens to point directly to L.A. International Airport. One busy Memorial Day weekend, Irv received a call from the control booth at Western Airlines. It seems the pilots had had fun over the years pointing out the pool and identifying it with the King of 31 Flavors. On this particular Memorial Day weekend, Irv had not flipped on the pool light (although it was pre-energy-crisis time). One pilot, "stacked up" and holding over Encino, called the tower and requested that the pool be lit as a bit of extra entertainment for his bored and fidgety passengers. Irv complied, naturally, and somehow (he won't say how) in next day's Los Angeles *Times* there appeared an item on the fact that Western pilots were using a certain cone-shaped pool to find their way into the L.A. Basin.

Here is a special treat for June—Lemon Custard Ice Cream Pie, the 1975 Ice Cream Show-Off Grand Prize winner. Now that it's over, we can talk about it. This recipe was so good it was a hands-down winner, but never did one innocent little lemon pie cause so many people so many hassles.

All judging must (of course) be impartial: no regard can be given to anything but the standards set down in the official rules and regulations. In those rules there is a list of about fifteen ice cream flavors which may be used to create recipes—primarily the flavors which are regulars in all BR stores. No other flavors can be accepted.

The grand-prize-winning recipe uses Lemon Custard Ice Cream, a flavor that was on the list but is not a store regular. Specifically, it (nor any other lemon ice cream) would not be in any store during the summer of 1975, when publicity on the winner would be breaking. What would be the point of sending out publicity on an exclusive recipe when people would have to go somewhere other than Baskin-Robbins to buy the ice cream to make it? But the publicity had to go out, so arrangements were made for special runs of Lemon Custard in all fifteen plants to provide every store with the flavor during the summer months.

The publicity photos were to be shot in San Francisco in early June, so a special batch of Lemon Custard was made and the ice cream sent up from Los Angeles. Two days later (just a few days before the scheduled photography session) it arrived back in Burbank: for some reason, nobody had freezer room for it in San Francisco. So it was packed in dry ice and sent special delivery by an air express service—the fastest, most direct way, right? Evidently not, because the ill-fated ice cream was next found aboard a disabled plane in Albuquerque, New Mexico. The plane had been bound from Los Angeles to San Francisco via Albuquerque and then Louisville, Kentucky. Finally, a third shipment made it to the photographer's studio in San Francisco, the dessert was made, shot, and everybody got to go home.

Oh, one other thing: Jeanne Randall, who submitted the recipe, had done so from her college address in Michigan. By the time the contest judging had been completed Jeanne was home in Corn-

Lemon Custard Ice Cream Pie

ing, New York. The phone number on her entry was her college dorm, full of summer students who had never heard of her. After four days of searching she was located.

A lot of hassle for one recipe . . . but anyone who tries it will agree it's worth the trouble. The short-bread crust combines with the tart lemon filling in a truly unusual cookie taste. When you top this off with the creamy Lemon Custard Ice Cream, plus whipped cream, you've really got a winner.

June 21st marks the beginning of summer—a perfect occasion to enjoy this light, creative dessert.

LEMON CUSTARD ICE CREAM PIE

6 tablespoons butter, softened
1 cup flour
¼ cup powdered sugar
2 eggs, beaten
¾ cup sugar
2 tablespoons flour
3 tablespoons lemon juice
1 teaspoon grated lemon rind
1 quart Baskin-Robbins Lemon Custard Ice Cream
1 cup whipping cream
4 thin slices of lemon, cut in half

Make a shortbread crust by blending the butter, 1 cup flour, and powdered sugar. Press mixture into the bottom and sides of a 9-inch greased pie pan. Bake in a 350-degree oven for 15 minutes (325 degrees for a glass pan). Mix eggs, sugar, 2 tablespoons flour, lemon juice, and rind. Pour over hot crust; bake 20 minutes longer. Remove from oven; let cool completely. Fill cooled crust with slightly softened ice cream. Place in freezer. Beat cream (with 2 tablespoons of sugar and 1 teaspoon vanilla) until stiff peaks form. Swirl whipped cream over top of pie. Garnish with twisted lemon slices. Freeze at least 3 hours. Remove from freezer about 10 minutes before serving to mellow. Makes 8 servings.

Jeanne Randall, Corning, New York (1975)

Gemini

Catch Gemini's attention (a major feat in itself) with these super different individual desserts combining nuts, ice cream, brown sugar, and cream cheese.

STRAWBERRY CHEESECAKE COOKIES

⅓ cup brown sugar, packed
½ cup chopped walnuts
1 cup flour
⅓ cup butter or margarine, melted
1 package (8 ounces) cream cheese, softened
¼ cup sugar
1 egg
1 tablespoon lemon juice
2 tablespoons cream or milk
1 teaspoon vanilla
1 quart Baskin-Robbins Fresh Strawberry Ice Cream

Mix brown sugar, nuts, and flour together in a bowl. Stir in melted butter and mix until light and crumbly. Set aside 1 cup of the mixture for a topping. Press remainder in the bottom of a buttered 8-inch square pan. Bake in a 350-degree oven for about 12 to 15 minutes. Beat cream cheese and the ¼ cup sugar until smooth. Mix in remaining ingredients, except ice cream. Spread evenly over the baked nut mixture. Top with remaining topping. Bake in oven another 25 minutes. Cool thoroughly. Spread the baked mixture with three-fourths of the ice cream. Cut into 16 squares. Freeze until ice cream is firm, about 3 hours. Makes 16 servings.

Pauletta V. Smith, West Lafayette, Indiana
(1975)

Here's a great variation of ham salad—served, quite naturally, with fresh pineapple and Baskin-Robbins' Pineapple Ultra Sherbet. Great for a hot summer day—afternoon or evening.

CHILLED PINEAPPLE SALAD

2 large pineapples
2 cups baked ham
4 stalks green celery, thinly sliced diagonally
6 green onions sliced

1 cup chilled bottled fruit salad dressing
1 pint Chilled Pineapple Sherbet

With sharp knife, cut crown from pineapple, then cut pineapple in two, crosswise. Form a shell from each half by removing meat, leaving walls and bottom about ½ inch thick. Discard core; cut pineapple into chunks. Gently toss pineapple chunks, ham, celery, and green onion slices together. Chill shells and ham mixture separately. (If desired, add 1 teaspoon celery seed to salad dressing.) At serving time, mix ham mixture and salad dressing. Spoon into pineapple shells. Top each with spoonfuls of Chilled Pineapple Sherbet.

Celebrate

June is a month for a lot of celebrations—weddings, showers, graduations. Outdoor gatherings call for a great bowl of punch, so we offer you several varieties here—enough to make everybody happy.

SPARKLING SHERBET PUNCH

You get all this color, sparkle, and great taste in two easy steps. And don't think one bowlful is going to do it. This punch is perfect for any June occasion. Spoon two quarts of Baskin-Robbins sherbet or ice, in large chunks, into a punch bowl. Any of the ultra sherbets—Chilled Strawberry, Chilled Peach, Chilled Pineapple—or plain Orange Sherbet or Champagne Grape Ice will be delicious. Pour four fifths of dry champagne over the sherbet, stir gently, and let stand five minutes. Makes 40 to 50 punch cup servings.

THE BERRIES MILK SHAKE

Make this simple milkshake just for the family or in larger quantities for a kids' summer party.

Slightly thaw one 10-ounce package of frozen raspberries; reserve 4 raspberries. Combine remaining raspberries, ¼ cup sugar, and 2 cups milk in blender. Blend five seconds; add 1 pint Baskin-Robbins Lemon Custard Ice Cream; blend just until smooth. Pour into 4 glasses; garnish with a dollop of whipped cream and a raspberry. Makes 4 servings.

Lelia F. Vacca, Tarrant, Alabama (1973)

CHOCOLATE CHERRY SUPER CHARGE

Here's a rich, refreshing drink that's suited to everybody, depending on whether or not you add the liqueur.

2 scoops Baskin-Robbins Burgundy Cherry Ice Cream
2 scoops Baskin-Robbins Chocolate Fudge Ice Cream
2 ounces creme de cacao, optional
1 can (12 ounces) black cherry soda, chilled

Place the scoops of ice cream in 2 tall glasses. If desired, pour creme de cacao over it. Fill glass with soda. Makes 2 servings.

Barbara Steinis, Portland, Oregon (1975)

CHAMPAGNE PUNCH

4 fifths champagne
Baskin-Robbins sherbet or
    ice of your choice

1 gallon Sauterne
2 large cans frozen lemon-
    ade concentrate

The day before, mix lemonade with Sauterne and freeze to make a slush. To serve, place slush in punch bowl and add soda and champagne. Float small scoops of Baskin-Robbins sherbets or ices (in complimentary colors). Generously serves about 12.

A Question of Quality

"A little neglect may breed great mischief . . . for want of a nail the shoe was lost; for want of a shoe the horse was lost; and for want of a horse the rider was lost."

—Benjamin Franklin,
Poor Richard's Almanac, 1758

Attention to detail, adherence to standards, and just plain *caring* is what goes into maintaining a quality product. Spend a day with the Baskin-Robbins quality people, and you'll *really* know why the ice cream tastes so good.

Ever wonder why a Coke you drink in Samoa tastes the same as the one you imbibe in San Francisco? Or why the Jamoca® Almond Fudge cone you lick while strolling Tokyo's Ginza tastes just as smooth and delicious as the one you bought three weeks ago in New York's Grand Central Station? Anyone would think that there'd be some sort of variation—one would be better than the other. After all, milk varies from place to place, climatic conditions are drastically different and, most important, people are different—we must allow for human error. Or must we?

Baskin-Robbins does more than allow for human error—they *prepare* for it, in order to prevent it. In all, there are fifteen plants manufacturing all those flavors from exclusive Baskin-Robbins formulas developed in Burbank by Les Moffitt, the Flavor Chef. Since Baskin-Robbins prides itself on its quality ice cream, not just the vast number of flavors, it is essential that all the ice cream, no matter where it is served, be creamy, just rich enough (but not overly rich), full of the best ingredients and, most of all, fresh.

In Burbank there's a white laboratory where Les Moffitt spends most of the time in his white lab coat. Les is responsible for development of all new flavors (a subject unto itself), and for quality assurance testing. Regularly throughout the year Les's lab is besieged by a group of men and women (also wearing lab coats for the occasion) who look pleasant enough. But these individuals (plant managers from each of the fifteen locations and various Baskin-Robbins executives, including Irv Robbins and President Bob Huducek) put on the masks of ogres when it comes to nit-picking ice cream.

First off, the ice cream samples (about twelve flavors each time) are requisitioned from a store in each plant area (the store owner must sign an affidavit attesting to the fact that the ice cream was just the same as what he received in his everyday shipment—no special testing samples allowed). The twelve samples from each area are flown, packed in dry ice, to headquarters.

Testing takes three days (nobody wants to overload his or her palate with taste sensations). Two flavors are tested each morning, two each afternoon. Smokers in the tasting group are forbidden to indulge their habit during the period. Nobody knows which ice cream belongs to whose plant, since all is carefully coded (different each time). The process begins. Les's assistant stands by with her score sheet, and fifteen cut gallons (a gallon slice of ice cream cut off the top of a three-gallon container) of Blueberries 'n Cream are presented at the judging table. All that purple and white swirliness is something to behold. And that's just what these scrutinizers do. They behold it for its appearance; thickness and quality of ribbon (that's the sweet, delicious blueberry mixture running through); texture; comparative color and body of the vanilla ice cream base; and overall ratio of ribbon to ice cream. Beside the fact that an ice cream tastes better with the proper balance of ingredients to ice cream (and at BR that always means a *lot* of ingredients), the super critics want it to look pretty when scooped up into a cone (a good ribbon balance means an appealing marbled effect in each scoop). When the eye has been satisfied and each sample has received its various appearance scores, the white coats dig daintily in with their pink sampling spoons. The ribbon is tasted and rated, then the vanilla base, and finally the whole conglomeration is rated. Iciness, creaminess, richness, fullness, texture, body, too much air, too little air . . . all these are terms that fly around the lab during taste testing. And this goes on for three days.

A final tally is made on each flavor for each plant and recommendations for improvement (should any be necessary) are sent out. In this way problem patterns can be easily and quickly detected and thus eliminated.

Father's Day

You can't go wrong on Father's Day with this double chocolate sundae.

SENOR PICO SUNDAE

12 "Mint Crispies," coarsely crushed (thin, crisp chocolate-covered mint candy)	4 large scoops Baskin-Robbins Chocolate Ice Cream

Put 1 tablespoon crushed candy in each of 4 sherbet glasses. Top with scoop of ice cream. Sprinkle each with remaining crushed candy. Makes 4 servings.

Tea Ice Cream?

Over the years the suggestions for various kinds of tea ice cream or sherbet have poured into Baskin-Robbins. For some reason no one has been able to come up with a concoction that tastes good enough to bother with—it's another one of those things that sounds interesting, but really doesn't turn out very well at all.

Cecelia Keas of Dubuque, Iowa, may have come up with one solution: she has combined iced tea with Lemon Custard Ice Cream and milk to produce a really refreshing and unusual drink. It's perfect for the many people out there who think ice cream and tea are a natural together.

LEMONY TEA CREAM

1½ cups cold milk
1 envelope (1.7 ounces) lemon-flavored iced tea mix

1 pint Baskin-Robbins Lemon Custard Ice Cream
Lemon slices, optional

Combine milk and iced tea mix in a bowl or blender. Add scoops of ice cream and blend to a thick consistency. Pour into 3 to 4 tall glasses and, if desired, garnish with thin slices of lemon. Makes 3 to 4 servings.

Cecelia Keas, Dubuque, Iowa (1975)

How About Burger 'n Fries?

In spite of the fact that Baskin-Robbins holds the record for greatest number and variety of ice cream flavors, the suggestions pour in from every quadrant. People stop Baskin-Robbins delivery trucks, they write in, call in, send telegrams; and many of the suggestions have been used, and most successfully. When anyone's suggestion goes into production, he or she receives a "Golden Scoop Award" showing Baskin-Robbins' appreciation. All suggestions, however, do not become realities (you will see why). Here are just a few:

Chop Suey	Lox 'n Bagels
Rum 'n Coke (or	Cannoli
Cubra Libre)	Candied Rumquat
Green Tea	Cheese 'n Crackers
Bacon Ripple	Liver 'n Onions
Boston Baked Bean	Green Goddess
Sweet Potato Pie	Kooky Cooky
(with potato pieces)	Koffee Klatchee
Yorkshire Pudding	Mocha Polka
Cactus Candy	Marlon Brandy
Dandelion Wine	New York Egg Creme

Candy Barr
Spiced Tea
Ice Tea
Blueberry Muffin
Chestnut
Guarana
Ugli Fruit
Sacher Torte
Moxie
Spice Cake
Tiger's Milk
Shoo-Fly Pie
Fortune Cookie
Wine Ripple
Hot Cross Bun
Turkish Taffy
Avocado Ice
Pop Tart
Peachy Ginger
Carrot Flip
Poppyseed Strudel
Ginger Beer Ice
Plum Pudding
Cold Buttered Rum
Midsummer's Night's
  Cream
Rococonut
Ciribiribin (cherries,
  berries, and bananas)

Prunella Whirl
Sub Lime
Clam Nectar
Oysters Rocky Road
Orange Julius
Fig Mint
Im Peach Mint
A Taste of Honey
Penny Candy
Gooseberry Gander
Dill Pickle
Cheddar Cheese
Billy Sundae
Southern Comfort
Zebra Cake
Jelly Bean
Cherri-O
Satur-Date
Tarzan and the Grapes
Lemeringue
Huckleberry Hound
Persimmon
Chutney Chip
Potato Chip
Brown Cow
It's a Mad, Mad, Mad,
  Mad Swirl
Custard's Last Stand

Apple Annie	Sweetie Pie
Sugar Foot	Vichyssoise Ice
U.S. Mint	Marrons Glacés
Animal Crackers	Fruit Curry

And you name it ... maybe you'll get a Golden Scoop Award!

Certainly the event most thought of in July is the commemoration of Independence Day, July 4. In the year of the American Bicentennial it is particularly appropriate to recall the following words, from John Adams's *Thoughts on Government*, written in 1776:

The second day (sic) of July, 1776, will be the most memorable epoch in the history of America. I am apt to believe that it will be celebrated by succeeding generations as the great anniversary festival. It ought to be commemorated as the day of deliverance, by solemn acts of devotion to God Almighty. It ought to be solemnized with pomp and parade, with shows, games, sports, guns, bells, bonfires and illuminations, from one end of this continent to the other, from this time forward forevermore. The happiness of society is the end of government.

Cancer

Home-oriented Cancerians will revel in this complicated Berry Banana dessert. It's a stay-at-home delight!

BERRY-BANANA ICE CREAM CAKE

1 package (18.5 ounces) banana or banana-nut cake mix
2 packages (10 ounces each) frozen strawberries, packed in syrup, partially thawed
1 tablespoon cornstarch
2 ripe bananas
1 quart Baskin-Robbins Banana Marshmallow Ice Cream
1 cup whipping or heavy cream
2 tablespoons powdered sugar
1 teaspoon vanilla
½ cup chopped walnuts or pecans

Prepare and bake cake mix according to package directions, using two 9-inch cake pans. Split each layer horizontally, to make two thin layers. Cut and remove center portion from two of the thin layers, leaving a 1½-inch ring of cake. (Reserve center portions for use at another time.) Put cake sections in freezer to chill. Drain juice from strawberries. Mix cornstarch with 2 tablespoons cold water; add to strawberry juice and bring to a boil, stirring constantly, until sauce is thickened and clear, about 2 minutes. Cool; add strawberries. Remove all cake layers from freezer. Lay each solid cake layer down, cut side up. Place a ring of cake on top of each solid layer. Spoon & spread, half of the ice cream into the hollow center of each cake sections. Slice one banana, and arrange on top of ice cream in one section of cake; spread half of the strawberry mixture on top of the other. Return both sections to freezer. Freeze 3 hours. Whip cream, adding powdered sugar and vanilla, until it holds its shape. Put the cake section with the sliced bananas on a cake plate, ice cream side up. Place second section on top of first, putting the strawberry-sauce side on top of the sliced bananas so that only cake is showing. Slice the second banana and arrange on top of cake. Frost entire cake with whipped cream. Swirl second half of strawberry mixture on top of cake; sprinkle nuts around sides. Freeze at least 3 hours. Let cake mellow in refrigerator 15 minutes before cutting into wedges. Makes 12 to 16 servings.

Barbara Peterson, Vicki Nelson, Evanston, Illinois (1975)

Independence Day

Following is a varied collection of ice cream confections to help every American celebrate not only the Bicentennial anniversary, but every succeeding day of independence.

SHRIMP AND SHERBET SALAD

Great for a summer supper or Sunday lunch. Lemon Peel Sherbet is so refreshing and delicious with shrimp.

12 butter lettuce leaves, washed, chilled	12 sprigs watercress (optional)
1 pound medium-large shrimp, chilled	Celery curls or avocado crescents
16 cherry tomatoes, halved and chilled	Baskin-Robbins Lemon Peel Sherbet
1 cup pineapple chunks or tidbits, drained, chilled	Oil and vinegar dressing, chilled

Lay three butter lettuce cups on each plate. Mound chilled shrimp in one, pineapple in the second. Arrange tomatoes and watercress in third cup. Place celery curls or avocado crescents between each lettuce cup. (To make celery curls, cut each celery stalk into 3-inch lengths. With paring knife, cut very thin, 1¼-inch slices at each end of celery pieces, leaving ½ inch intact in center. Place immediately in ice water. Refrigerate, covered, at least an hour. Drain well on paper towels.) Place large scoop (or rosette) of Lemon Peel Sherbet in center of plate. Serve immediately. Pass dressing. Makes 4 servings.

FRESH FRUIT DAIQUIRIS

½ cup light rum
½ cup crushed ice

3 large scoops Baskin-Robbins Daiquiri Ice

Place these three ingredients in blender container. Then add *one* of the fruits listed below:

4 large ripe strawberries, or
10 unpeeled apricot halves, or

½ cup raspberries, or
1 ripe banana, or
2 pear halves, canned or fresh

Turn blender to low, then to high; whirr just until blended. Pour into stemmed glasses; garnish with fresh mint or pieces of fruit. Makes 3 to 4 servings.

MELON BOAT SALAD WITH MANGO SHERBET

1 large cantaloupe, honeydew, or Spanish melon
1 box strawberries, hulled and halved

2 large oranges, sectioned
2 bananas, peeled, scored, sliced diagonally
1 pint Baskin-Robbins Mango Sherbet

Quarter melon; remove seeds. With melon-baller cut out as many balls as possible. Scrape out rest of melon with spoon to form shell. Gently mix orange segments and banana slices. Refrigerate shells and fruit. At serving time, place shells on plates and arrange melon balls and fruit in each. Top with a generous scoop of Mango Sherbet. If desired, serve with hot buttered biscuits, filled with thin slices of ham. Makes 4 servings.

SUMMER PEACH SIPPER

Use this sippin' desert, served in some stemmed glasses, to wind up a good dinner any time of the year.

1 package (10 ounces) frozen peaches, slightly thawed
¼ cup unsweetened pineapple juice, chilled

¾ cup milk
1 pint Baskin-Robbins Vanilla Ice Cream

Place peaches with juice, pineapple juice, and milk in blender. Cover; blend on high speed about 5 seconds. Add ice cream; blend just until thick and smooth. Pour into four glasses. If desired, garnish with peach slices. Makes 4 servings.

Bess Myers, Odessa, Texas (1973)

Vegetable Ice Cream?

One common flavor suggestion is the flavor based on some sort of vegetable. Cucumber sherbet, green chile ice, eggplant ripple . . . you name it. But the only one ever tried, and actually eaten, was Ketchup Ice Cream.

Milt Josefsberg, TV writer extraordinaire (Bob Hope and The Lucy Show being among his many credits) and longtime buddy of Irv Robbins and Burt Baskin, is the ketchup freak of all times. He makes it into sandwiches, sloshes it onto meat and vegetables, drowns ice cream with it, and even adds it to various kinds of packaged soup.

His two ice cream buddies, upon opening their Encino, California, store (Milt lives in Encino), paid special tribute to their illustrious friend by concocting a batch of Ketchup Ice Cream—ten full gallons. The Encino store featured it opening day. Milt made an appearance and since nobody else wanted any, he got to take it all home. Says Milt,

"My wife and I tried to eat it plain, we tried to use it as aspic, we tried to get the dog to eat it, we even tried putting ketchup on it. Finally we tried to flush it down the toilet and the resultant plumbing bill was over $100." Milt's advice to flavor inventors: Stick with fruits and nuts and candies—vegetables just don't make it, even for a ketchup nut.

Mrs. Marion Stephens of Texas City, Texas, would disagree with Milt, and her Show Off entry proves it. She suggests taking two cups each of finely chopped fresh tomatoes, celery, and carrots, one cup of finely chopped cucumber, and adding it to one-half gallon of softened Baskin-Robbins Vanilla Ice Cream. She then puts it back in the freezer and serves it right out of the original ice cream container. It's called "Garden of Eden." Who knows?

July 14—Bastille Day

NAPOLEONS

These are a delicious variation on the traditional French pastry—the perfect dessert to celebrate France's proudest day.

1 package (10 ounces) frozen patty shells (6 shells)

1 quart Baskin-Robbins Pistachio Almond Fudge or Pistachio Almond Ice Cream

1 jar (9 ounces) Baskin-Robbins Hot Fudge, warmed

Green pistachio nuts, chopped

Thaw patty shells in refrigerator. On lightly floured surface, lay out shells 2 wide and 3 deep. Roll out to a 8″ × 12″ rectangle; cut into eight 3″ × 4″ rectangles with fluted pastry cutter. Lay on ungreased baking sheet. Bake in 400-degree oven for 20 minutes or until deep golden brown. Remove to rack. Cool. Split pastries in half lengthwise. On bottom pastry layer, spread ice cream in a thick layer. Replace top and freeze. Repeat with remaining pastry. Just before serving, spoon warmed hot fudge over top of pastry. Garnish with chopped nuts. Makes 8 servings.

Frances Raab, Chelmsford, Massachusetts (1975)

Summer Breakfast

Bacon and eggs sounds pretty uninviting on a hot July morning, so try something different. Make up a bunch of crisp waffles and top them with Baskin-

Robbins Oregon Blackberry, Fresh Strawberry, or Fresh Peach Ice Cream. Or try this special nutritious summer liquid breakfast:

BREAKFAST BANANZA

1 pint Baskin-Robbins Fresh Strawberry Ice Cream	¼ cup frozen concentrated orange juice, undiluted
1 ripe banana, peeled, quartered	1 tablespoon wheat germ
4 eggs	2 cups milk

Scoop Fresh Strawberry Ice Cream, or a Baskin-Robbins banana-flavored ice cream, into blender; add remaining ingredients. Blend on high speed just until smooth. Pour into glasses. Makes 4 servings.

Carolyn H. Johnson, Glendale, California (1973)

Pink Bubble Gum

After the Goody Goody Gum Drop episode everybody at BR was scared to death of Bubble Gum Ice Cream, but kids were clamoring for it. Finally they developed a bubble gum that could be put into the ice cream without hardening to rock texture, and Pink Bubble Gum was born. It is an overly pink, sick-sweet concoction that tastes like molten Bazooka, but kids love it . . . everywhere but in Washington State, where the legislature passed a bill outlawing it, and we think maybe it's because kids get bored with chewing the gum and can always find another obnoxious place to deposit it.

Lunar Cheesecake

Where were you on the evening of July 20, 1969? Chances are pretty good that, like most people (in the United States anyway), you were perched on the edge of your chair in front of a TV screen waiting to see the first man take his first step on the moon. The seventies have brought with them a lot of second thoughts about the necessity of space

exploration when our own world needs so much improvement, but Apollo XI was an exciting and incredible culmination of the Space Age sixties; perhaps it's a shame we have had to set our sights lower during this decade, but optimists tell us if we got ourselves into some kind of temporary mess on the planet, we can get ourselves out of it, and we will.

The first step on the moon, regardless of how much energy or money it took to become a reality, offered a few moments of expanded vision even to the narrow-minded (although there were those cynics who believed the whole thing was taking place on a sound-stage somewhere). Irv Robbins, being anything but narrow-minded, not only followed the space program with gusto, he based a whole new ice cream flavor on it. Being the optimist that he is, Robbins had a good feeling about Apollo XI. "What a great thing it would be," he thought in his highly promotional brain, "if we could offer a new flavor in all of our stores across the country just as soon as the first man has walked on the moon."

So was born Lunar Cheesecake, a whole new flavor created just for the occasion and kept entirely under wraps until Neil Armstrong lumbered down from that spidery looking craft onto that not-too-cheesy-looking lunar surface. As soon as Baskin-Robbins store owners had drawn a breath, those that were still open plastered up colorful new signs they had received a few days before to celebrate the success of the mission with their very own new flavor, an unusual combination of Baskin-Robbins' exclusive Cheesecake Ice Cream (colored green, naturally) and laced with a marshmallow ribbon. The timing was perfect, the flavor was a hit, and everybody was happy.

But what would have happened if something had gone wrong with the Apollo mission? All that ice cream, all those signs, all that effort? "Naturally we're not polyannas," says Robbins, "but we were banking, as everyone else was, on the success of the mission. If something had gone wrong, I guess we could have held onto the ice cream and eventually renamed it. If you think negatively, though, nothing ever gets accomplished."

August is the height of the summer, the apogee of the year, when more things bloom and come to fruition than any other time. The weather isn't always great, but it is generally a very rich, full time.

Driving cross-country through the Midwest in August is a sensual experience. The flatlands, grey and dull in winter, are at the full stage of pregnancy. Corn and other crops brim over the landscape; the heat and humidity are almost tropical, and ice cream is a welcome treat from Seattle to Bangor.

Toward the end of the month an urgency sets in as the light begins to speak of fall and the coming winter. The days begin noticeably to shorten, and while cooler days will be welcome, they are nevertheless a reminder that another summer, and thus another year, is passing. The current year will never again be so affluent as it is during August.

Leo

Splashy, dramatic Leo could stand for nothing less than the showiest of ice cream desserts. This variation of fondue—little cream puffs filled with various flavors of ice cream and then dipped into the most incredible chocolate sauce you've ever tasted—ought to be spectacular enough for even the grandest of Leos.

HEAVENLY ICE CREAM PUFF FONDUE

This recipe was the grand prize winner in the 1973 Show Off contest.

Here's a real show-stopper for a celebration, dinner party, dessert buffet, or teen-ager's fondue party.

Fill tiny cream puffs with ice cream and stash them in the freezer ahead of time. To serve, warm thick chocolate sauce in fondue pot or chafing dish, then everybody spears the puffs on forks and dips and twirls in the sauce.

36 miniature cream puffs, bakery or homemade (recipe follows)
1 pint Baskin-Robbins Jamoca® Ice Cream*
2 cups Chocolate Fondue Sauce (recipe follows)
1 pint Baskin-Robbins Burgundy Cherry Ice Cream*
1 pint Baskin-Robbins Chocolate Mint Ice Cream*

Cut tops off puffs; pull out any filaments of dough to form hollow shells. Fill and mound six puffs (using a melon-ball cutter or teaspoon) with one flavor of ice cream. Press tops into ice cream; place in freezer. Fill six more puffs with first flavor. Freeze. Repeat with second and third flavors. Continue until desired number of puffs are filled, allowing 6 to a serving. When all are frozen, place in a plastic bag; freeze until served. To serve: Gently heat chocolate fondue sauce in a fondue pot or decorative skillet; arrange frozen, filled puffs on plates. Each guest spears a puff with fondue fork, dips into the sauce, and swirls to coat. If desired, small bowls

* Or any 3 or more of your favorite Baskin-Robbins flavors.

of flaked coconut, chopped pecans, and chocolate
bits can be arranged around sauce in which to dip
the chocolate-coated puffs. Makes 6 servings.

Chocolate Fondue Sauce

1 can (14 ounces)
  sweetened condensed
  milk
1 package (12 ounces)
  semisweet chocolate
  bits
½ cup milk

1 jar (7 ounces) marsh-
  mallow creme or 1
  package (6¼ ounces)
  miniature marshmal-
  lows (3¾ cups)
1 teaspoon vanilla

Combine all ingredients in saucepan. Heat over
medium heat, stirring, just until mixture is smooth
and warmed through. Sauce can be made ahead, refrigerated, and reheated. (It will keep indefinitely in
the refrigerator.) Add a little milk if sauce becomes
too thick. Makes 4 cups.

Miniature Cream Puffs

(Miniature cream puffs can be ordered, in advance,
from many bakeries.) Preheat oven to 375 degrees.
In small saucepan slowly bring ½ cup water, ¼ cup
butter or margarine, and ¼ teaspoon salt to a boil.
Turn heat low; stir in ½ cup all-purpose flour all at

once. Beat with a wooden spoon until mixture leaves sides of pan and forms into a small, compact ball. Remove from heat, then add 2 eggs, beating until smooth. Drop dough, by half teaspoonfuls, the size of a nickel, 2 inches apart, onto an ungreased baking sheet. Bake 25 to 30 minutes or until puffed and golden. Cool away from draft. Makes about 36 miniature cream puffs, 1½ inches in diameter.

Laurie H. Freedman, Brooklyn, New York (1973)

Summer Evening

Cool off a summer evening with this unusual skewered variation of fresh fruit salad. A great light supper.

SANGRIA ICE AND FRUIT KABOB

Flavored like the delicious wine punch that originated in Spain, the sophisticated ice is an elegant addition to a fresh fruit salad.

4 large strawberries
1 small cantaloupe
8 honeydew melon balls
2 bananas, peeled
Butter lettuce

1 pint Baskin-Robbins Sangria Ice
4 bamboo or decorated skewers

(Wash and chill all fruit, except banana and lettuce.) At serving time peel cantaloupe. Cut in half, remove seeds; cut each half in two into a crescent shape. Arrange lettuce on 4 serving plates. Thread, on each skewer, a half strawberry, melon ball, cantaloupe crescent, strawberry half, a diagonally cut chunk of banana, melon ball; lay on the lettuce. Just before serving, press a large scoop of Sangria Ice on the end of each skewer; serve immediately. Pass cheese crisps or dark bread and butter sandwiches and salad dressing, if desired. Makes 4 servings.

This easy-to-do dessert is made with crunchy ice cream cone crust, flavored with dark chocolate and almonds.

ICE CREAM CONE PIE

1 dozen Baskin-Robbins
   Ice Cream Sugar
   Cones, crushed
3 tablespoons toasted slivered almonds
2 tablespoons butter

½ package (6 ounces)
   semisweet chocolate
   bits
1 quart Baskin-Robbins
   Chocolate Mint Ice
   Cream

(Reserve ¼ cup crushed cones for garnish.) Combine remaining crushed cones and almonds in a mixing bowl. Gently melt butter and 3 ounces of chocolate bits; pour over crushed cone mixture. Mix thoroughly to coat crushed cones. Press into bottom and sides of a 9-inch pie pan. Chill until firm. Fill pie shell with slightly softened ice cream; garnish with the reserved crushed cones. Freeze. Makes 6 to 8 servings.

J. W. Battaglia, El Paso, Texas (1973)

The Story of Baskin and Robbins

Maybe some people have wondered from time to time how a company like Baskin-Robbins ever got to be so recognized and relied upon. Baskin-Robbins, after only thirty-one years in business, is well on its way to being an institution, almost a household word. There's got to be a story behind all those flavors and all that fun.

Irv Robbins has been around milk and dairy products since before he can remember; his dad was a successful dairy owner in Tacoma, Washington, and he even had one or two ice cream stores back when Irv was a kid. There was something called "Court C" in an alleyway behind one of downtown

Tacoma's busy department stores, and it did a land-office business selling ice cream and buttermilk. Irv recalls business people bringing in their bag lunches to sit on the wooden school chair/desks, sip buttermilk with their lunch, and enjoy some ice cream for dessert. He also recalls a sense of satisfaction in working in such a store (he began around age 14, afternoons and weekends) where people came in to enjoy themselves, not as a duty or out of necessity. "It struck me there was a great difference between the experience of coming to an ice cream store and, for example, going to the pharmacy for a prescription or even going to the grocery store," Irv says. "People seemed to be coming into our Court C store for a little break, for some relaxation and fun. You can bet I was thankful to be working there and not someplace else."

From his father, Irv Robbins learned the ins and outs of the dairy business. In addition to working at the retail end, young Irv helped out around the factory where the ice cream and other products were produced. In his late teens he began to experiment with some exotic flavors, but little did he imagine that some two decades later his name would become synonymous with the word flavor in the ice cream business.

At the same time Irv developed a sense of marketing which would also contribute greatly to his later success. Calling on grocery and variety stores, customers of his father's dairy, the young man made every attempt to persuade these merchants to display signs advertising his product. But he soon realized that he could do a whole snow job on the grocer, who would then acquiesce and put up the sign, but as soon as Irv walked out of the store another salesman for another product would arrive and talk up the merits of advertising his product. "What I recognized from this experience," Irv recalls, "is that the grocer is in business, naturally, just to sell a lot of merchandise. He doesn't really care whether it is *my* merchandise or that of the next fellow." Thus was born in Irv's head the concept of the specialty ice cream store—a store that sells only ice cream, no soft drinks, no gum, no cigarettes. This principle has been challenged over the thirty-one years of BR's history, but it has never been changed. The reason is that it *works*.

Irv's past is not a checkered one: throughout college he worked in the same business—he never really drifted away from dairy-related work. He was stationed in California during World War II and made up his mind to settle there with his wife and newly arrived child when the war ended. With a few thousand dollars in his pocket, he set out from Washington state in the summer of 1945 to make his fortune. Wife Irma and the baby would stay close to home in Washington until some promise broke over the horizon.

None did. Irv's dream of ice cream began to melt as he realized the war had created a tremendous building shortage. He hunted for over a month for a store location in Palo Alto, San Jose, and the whole San Francisco peninsula area. Finally, in need of supplies from several Southern California firms, he packed a small suitcase and drove to Los Angeles, thinking the trip might change his luck.

Never one to be pessimistic, Robbins found all the supplies for his ice cream store and ordered them, telling the vendors to hold delivery until he had an address to send to. Hope was high at war's end, and apparently none of these companies felt particularly threatened by the obvious precariousness of Irv's credit situation.

Mission accomplished, Robbins set out in the wee hours for the return to Northern California and great things to come. Passing the legendary Forest Lawn Cemetery, then billed as the burying place of the stars, he decided to have a look, but it was only 6:30 and the place didn't open till 9:00. His determination to see the stars' graves was evidently strong: he thought he'd wait. And while waiting he'd find some breakfast and poke around the area. Before he could do either of the above, his eyes were struck by a large *For Rent* sign in a rather spacious, triangular store at the corner of Adams and Palmer in Glendale, an incorporated city about seven miles from downtown Los Angeles. He waited to apply at the rattan furniture store next door, as the sign instructed, and by a few minutes after 9:00, the store was his. He never went back to San Jose, just sent for his things. Three weeks later—December 7, 1945, the first "Snowbird" Ice Cream and frozen food store opened; first day's take, around $35.00, $23.00 of it from a friendly cousin who happened to live in Glendale.

This first store was a far cry from what we think of as Baskin-Robbins today, but within a few months of its opening, it did sport many of the unique qualities: number one, there were twenty-one flavors, many more than most people had ever thought of, and each one was advertised periodically by a colorful, cartoonlike sign. The ice cream was good, too, although undoubtedly not quite so good as BR's today, since it was manufactured by somebody else and Irv pasted the Snowbird label on; after all, with only one store, who could afford his own ice cream plant? There were even taste spoons, and of course those strange school desks.

Just after Irv had opened his second store, his brother-in-law, Burton "Butch" Baskin, appeared on the scene. Butch had been in the South Seas during the war thinking up crazy ice cream flavors to make in his commandeered ice cream freezer, and now he was in Southern California to continue the career that had been interrupted by the war. Coming from a long line of retailers of quality

171

menswear, Baskin had been operating a small haberdashery shop at Chicago's Palmer House Hotel prior to 1941. It was his intention to open a fine men's store on Beverly Drive in fledgling Beverly Hills . . . until pal Irv convinced him that ice cream was where it was at.

The two young men wanted to enter immediately into a binding partnership, but Irv's father, Ernie Robbins (luckily) got to them first. He said that each of them would have ideas he'd want to put into practice, and sometimes these ideas might differ greatly. He added that if either man gave into the other's wishes too often, resentment would occur and the entire partnership would eventually be weakened. "Follow the same basic principles," he said, "but go with your own separate ideas for a while. That way, only one person will be responsible for each mistake. If, after you've got the kinks out, you still want to be partners, do it."

Obviously, they did. Ernie Robbins did not live to see the fruition of his sage advice, and he certainly would have been proud. For about five years the two men worked somewhat independently, although Irv now admits they were always working toward some common goal. What the goal was, at that point, neither of them really knew—very often it was keeping away from bankruptcy, as it usually is with any new business.

But Baskin and Robbins did a lot more than keep

the wolf from the door. They kept adding stores, and finally realized they had too many to oversee properly by themselves. Says Irv, "Suddenly we had more stores, greater volume, but our overall earnings were dropping. Burt and I couldn't be in all the stores all the time and, after all, it was our baby, and nobody else's. We had great people working for us, don't get me wrong, but it just didn't mean as much to them as it did to us. Even if we gave them an interest beyond the salary, it still didn't make it. That's when we came up with the ownership idea, to give people a proprietary interest in their own business. We set them up, supplied all the know-how, the inroads, the systems. It was the concept of franchising, and we didn't even know it."

After they began franchising, and after they had become Baskin-Robbins 31 Flavors Ice Cream, things began to really blossom. They bought an old ice cream factory in Burbank, a plant that is functional to this day (in 1975 it produced over seven million gallons of premium ice cream), and it is now just one of fifteen plants in the world making Baskin-Robbins Ice Cream. In 1959 they began to move out of California, and by 1965 Baskin-Robbins had hit New York, Washington, and many other parts of the East, the Midwest, and the South. When asked if he had been afraid to implement BR in the colder climates, Irv Robbins simply said, "It's always summertime in your living room." Must be, because today there are 1500 stores in the United States alone.

The history goes on, but apart from the early days it is primarily a success story, a tale of expansion, buy/sell kind of stuff, not that interesting, except for the fact that the concepts—those of selling a quality product on an exclusive basis with more variety and excitement than anybody else—worked. Baskin-Robbins really doesn't have any competition, because there is no other national (international) chain of ice cream stores in existence.

Our 50th and Most Exotic State

On August 15, 1959, Hawaii became our 50th state. To commemorate that historic event we give you two very special, very different prize-winning desserts.

BAKED HAWAII

Fill a fresh pineapple shell with pineapple chunks, Burgundy Cherry, and Fresh Coconut Ice Cream and place in the freezer several days ahead. Just before serving, top the filled shell with meringue and brown quickly in the oven.

1 large ripe pineapple	1 pint Baskin-Robbins Burgundy Cherry Ice Cream
¼ cup sugar	
1 pint Baskin-Robbins Fresh Coconut Ice Cream	1 teaspoon rum flavoring
	Meringue (recipe below)

Lay pineapple on its side. With a sharp, heavy knife cut off a one-half-inch slice lengthwise. Leave green-leaved crown intact. With a thin, sharp knife, cut out fruit, leaving a shell. Cut out core from fruit; discard core. Cut 2 cups of fruit into bite-size pieces; mix with sugar and rum flavoring. Let stand 30 minutes. (Remainder of fruit can be used for salads, compotes, etc.) Wrap leaves of pineapple with foil; freeze for 30 minutes. Drain sweetened fruit. Remove shell from freezer; half fill with slightly softened Fresh Coconut Ice Cream, or any other Baskin-Robbins coconut-flavored ice cream; spoon drained rum-pineapple pieces evenly over ice cream. Fill remainder of shell with slightly softened Burgundy Cherry Ice Cream. Freeze for at least 2 hours.

To make meringue: Beat 2 eggs with ½ teaspoon lemon juice and ½ teaspoon rum flavoring until frothy. Gradually beat in 4 tablespoons sugar, a little at a time. Continue beating until stiff and glossy. Remove filled pineapple from freezer; lay on small cutting board or baking sheet. Completely cover and seal ice cream and edge of shell with meringue. (If desired, freeze up to 24 hours.) Bake in a preheated 500-degree oven, on lowest rack, about

2 minutes or until meringue is delicately browned. Remove foil from leaves. Slice, with heavy, sharp knife or electric knife through meringue, ice cream, and shell into one-inch slices. Makes 6 to 8 servings.

Ann and Richard Dickinson, Indianapolis, Indiana (1973)

HAWAII SPECIAL SUNDAE

4 tablespoons butter	1 cup firmly packed brown sugar
1 cup salted macadamia nuts, coarsely chopped	1 quart Baskin-Robbins Fresh Banana or Fresh Coconut Ice Cream
1 cup whipping or heavy cream	

Melt butter in saucepan, mix in nuts; heat, stirring occasionally, until lightly toasted. Stir in brown sugar and cream. Bring just to a boil and simmer until blended, stirring constantly. Let cool slightly. Spoon warm sauce over individual scoops of ice cream. (Sauce can be made ahead, refrigerated, and warmed just before serving.) Makes 8 servings.

Miriam Hartigan, Wheaton, Illinois (1975)

About Burt Baskin

Burt Baskin was an enterprising young man from the Midwest. His family had a long history in the retailing business (men's clothes); in fact, today

176

members of the Baskin family still operate some of the finest men's shops in the country in Ottawa, Illinois, called, appropriately, Baskin's.

Burt Baskin started out in retailing with a small shop inside Chicago's famous Palmer House Hotel. It was a successful shop, catering to formal wear needs and, ultimately, to the dress needs of military personnel. World War II had arrived. Baskin joined the Navy and pretty soon found himself in the South Seas working supply detail for a land operation. Being something of a wheeler dealer, and always very much of good joe type, Baskin figured a way to get an ice cream freezer into his outfit by trading somebody else's jeep (shades of "MASH"). Evidently nobody ever missed the jeep, but a lot of people noticed the ice cream freezer, since Baskin had the ingenuity to embellish the bland wartime powdered ice cream base with large, juicy native tropical fruits and nuts. Thus was born the flavor concept which much later became an American standard in the form of Baskin-Robbins 31 Flavors Ice Cream Stores.

Summer Refreshers

Baskin and Robbins wouldn't want anybody to let the summer just peter out (ice cream-wise, anyway). August usually goes out with a bang in the heat department, so just before we plunge headlong into September, which just happens to be Chocolate Month, let's stop and look at a few more summer refreshers.

One beautifully simple idea for an end-of-summer beach party is to take a large, wide-mouthed thermos and fill it about three-quarters of the way up with whole, ice-cold milk. Add enough scoops of your favorite flavor of Baskin-Robbins Ice Cream to fill. Stash the thermos in the car with other goodies and head for the beach. Give it a shake every once in a while, and by the time you get ready to eat, you'll have a great natural milkshake!

Bananas and ice cream are a natural together, and super refreshing for hot summer days. Here are three great new recipes to try.

BANANA MELBA

1 package (10 ounces) frozen raspberries, defrosted	½ cup sugar
	⅛ teaspoon salt
	1 quart Baskin-Robbins Banana Rocky Road Ice Cream
½ cup currant jelly	
2 teaspoons cornstarch	

Put defrosted raspberries through sieve into saucepan. Add jelly and heat until dissolved. Combine cornstarch, sugar, and salt; stir into fruit mixture. Heat, stirring, until thickened. Place scoops of

Banana Rocky Road Ice Cream into sherbet glasses. Top with warm raspberry sauce. Makes 8 servings.

DOUBLE BANANA SPLIT

Split peeled bananas lengthwise; place three halves, with cut side up, on a pretty plate. Top with two large scoops of Banana Rocky Road Ice Cream, or any other Baskin-Robbins banana-flavored ice cream. Top one scoop with crushed pineapple, second scoop with thawed frozen raspberries.

ROYAL HAWAIIAN SUNDAE

1 can (8½ ounces) crushed pineapple
1 tablespoon butter or margarine
2 teaspoons cornstarch
2 tablespoons flaked coconut
3 tablespoons brown sugar
2 teaspoons lemon juice
1 quart Baskin-Robbins Banana Rocky Road Ice Cream

Mix first four ingredients in saucepan. Cook over medium heat until thickened, about 5 minutes. Stir in coconut. Serve warm over scoops of Baskin-Robbins Banana Rocky Road Ice Cream, or any other Baskin-Robbins banana-flavored ice cream, in your prettiest compotes. Makes 8 servings.

SEPTEMBER

The beginning of September is technically the end of summer because, although autumn doesn't officially begin until the 21st, there is a psychological end of summer on Labor Day: school generally reopens shortly thereafter and once all the kids are back under one roof, nothing seems quite the same (sigh!). Luckier parents take vacations by themselves, summer resorts begin to close their doors, and things in general seem to settle down a little bit.

This writer recalls the passing of Labor Day very specifically from about fifteen years' experience with a resort called Falmouth Heights, Massachusetts. Summers there were bustling but pleasurable, in a family-owned guest house known as The Gladstone Inn. Labor Day weekend was one of the most crowded (and most revenue-producing) of the season, and of course it all had to end Monday night.

At two o'clock Monday afternoon the beaches, parking lots, and rooms would be jammed; bags had been packed and cars were gassed up, but everybody was waiting just till the last moment to soak up those final life-giving rays. By six o'clock the entire community had become a virtual ghost town: nothing left on the beach but litter, nothing in the parking lots but some grease stains and melted ice cream cones, and nothing in the rooms but beds still unstripped of soiled linen. The summer had ended, and a walk along the empty boardwalk was a chilling realization for a young kid whose duty it was to be sitting in a classroom more than fifty miles away at eight o'clock next morning.

September was the month Baskin-Robbins chose several years ago to stage a Chocolate Lovers' Festival, when fifteen different varieties of chocolate ice cream were featured in all stores. There's nothing better than good old chocolate to ward off those "Summer's over and it's back-to-school-time blues."

Virgo

Any Virgo who doesn't like this dessert isn't true to his sign: it's clean, pure, and delicious. It hardly even requires any clean-up, since the coconut shell serves as a dish.

VIRGIN'S DELIGHT

2 coconuts, drained and halved
1 quart Baskin-Robbins Coconut Chocolate Chip or Coconut Almond Fudge Ice Cream
1½ cups toasted flaked coconut
1 small jar pineapple topping for ice cream

To select fresh coconuts: Choose ones that are relatively heavy. A larger amount of coconut milk inside indicates freshness. To prepare coconut shells: thoroughly wash and dry outside of coconuts. Punch 3 holes in the end, where dark indentations appear. Drain coconut milk into a container. Refrigerate or freeze for other uses. Secure coconut in a vise or similar holder. Using a large carpenter's handsaw, saw coconut in half—the shell is very tough. Coconut meat may be left in shell or removed, as desired. Fill each coconut half with ice cream. Press gently into shells level with edge. Cover each with foil. Freeze at least 3 hours. Fifteen minutes before serving, place filled shells in refrigerator. To serve, spoon pineapple topping on each shell. Sprinkle generously with toasted coconut. Garnish with flowers, tiny paper umbrellas. Surround each serving with a paper lei. Makes 4 servings.

Melanie Morel, Baton Rouge, Louisiana (1975)

Labor Day

Look forward to the pleasures of autumn on Labor Day with this unusual fresh apple dessert.

GINGER APPLEMON ALASKA

1 quart Baskin-Robbins Lemon Custard Ice Cream	6 tablespoons sugar
	1 egg
	1½ teaspoons ginger
⅓ cup butter or margarine, melted	½ teaspoon cinnamon
	½ teaspoon ground cloves
⅔ cup firmly packed brown sugar	¼ teaspoon nutmeg
	½ cup molasses
2 cups sliced fresh apples	1 cup flour, plus 2 tablespoons
2 tablespoons raisins	¼ teaspoon salt
1 teaspoon cinnamon	4 egg whites
¼ cup butter or margarine	½ cup powdered sugar

Line an 8-inch mixing bowl with foil. Pack with slightly softened ice cream. Freeze 3 hours. Mix the melted butter and brown sugar in bottom of a 9-inch cake pan. Cover with apple slices; sprinkle with raisins and 1 teaspoon cinnamon. Cream the ¼ cup butter with sugar and egg. Blend in the 4 spices. Alternately add molasses and flour mixed with salt. Mix well. Spread over apple mixture. Bake in a 350-degree oven about 35 minutes or until done. Turn out, upside down, on an oven-proof serving plate; cool. Chill. Beat egg whites until stiff, gradually beating in powdered sugar. Unmold ice cream on top of chilled, upside-down cake. Cover ice cream with meringue, sealing to cake. Bake in a preheated 450-degree oven, about 3 minutes, until lightly brown. Serve immediately. Makes 8 to 12 servings.

Mary Allard, San Antonio, Texas (1975)

Back to School

These are two great treats to give the kids after school any time, but what better time than those first warm days when their minds are on anything but the three R's? Both recipes are easy and delicious.

MIGHTY FINE FIVE

10 graham crackers
5 tablespoons nutty
   peanut butter
5 tablespoons currant
   jelly

1 pint Baskin-Robbins
   French Vanilla Ice
   Cream

Spread 5 graham crackers with peanut butter, five with currant jelly. Cover each peanut butter graham with a small scoop of ice cream. Top the ice cream with a jellied graham, jelly side down. Freeze. Makes 5 servings.

Mary Santucci, Concord, New Hampshire (1973)

ISLANDS IN THE SEA

1 large package (5.5 ounces) chocolate fudge pudding mix
3 cups milk
1 pint Baskin-Robbins Burgundy Cherry Ice Cream
1 pint Baskin-Robbins Chocolate Mint Ice Cream
1 pint Baskin-Robbins Jamoca® Almond Fudge Ice Cream

Cook pudding mix, with milk, according to package directions. Cool slightly until warm, not hot. Pour the warm pudding into eight attractive deep dessert dishes or compotes. Place a small scoop of each of the ice creams on top of the warm pudding. Serve immediately. Makes 8 servings.

Eva A. Yorke, Syracuse, New York (1975)

Chocolate

In a country that is as hedonistic as it is diet-conscious, there is probably one food or snack item that stands apart from all the rest. When all is said and done, who wouldn't prefer something chocolate to a pizza, or a hamburger and fries, or a bag of Fritos? Cocoa, chocolate bars, brownies, chocolate chip cookies, devil's food cake and, of course, chocolate ice creams have become such a part of our lives one would never dream that it has only been during the last hundred years that chocolate has been generally produced or consumed. And thirty percent of the world's cocoa beans are processed for consumption in the United States—Americans are the chocolate freaks of all times! Just think of all the different chocolate ice creams there are, many of them developed exclusively by Baskin-Robbins: Chocolate Fudge, Chocolate Chip, Chocolate Mint, Chocolate Almond, German Chocolate Cake, Jamoca® Almond Fudge, Chocolate Cheesecake, Mandarin Chocolate Sherbet, Fudge Brownie, Bittersweet Chocolate, Here Comes Da Fudge . . . about ninety Baskin-Robbins chocolate variations in all. Enough so that for several years BR has set aside a special month during the year when fifteen (count 'em, fifteen) chocolate flavors have been available all at once in all the stores! And after the month had ended each time, we got letters from chocolate nuts lambasting us and saying, "You big dummies, why not make *every* month chocolate month." There are some people who wouldn't consider eating ice cream unless it contained chocolate in one form or another.

So, knowing all this, it is even harder to believe that chocolate as we know it has been around such a short time. Let's take a closer look at chocolate and how it makes its way to our salivating palates.

The encyclopedia defines *cocoa* as a tropical tree, not to be confused with the coconut palm or South American coca shrub, whose leaves produce cocaine (certainly not!). The cocoa-producing tree is another native of Central and South America, however.

The trees will grow to forty feet, but for cultivation purposes they are generally kept somewhere between fifteen and twenty-five feet. Small, pink-hued blossoms on trunk and many of the broad branches precede green, podlike fruit, which develop through a yellow-orange stage to a ripe reddish-purple. The mature pods resemble enlarged cantaloupes or cucumbers (average 6–14 inches long and 2–5 inches in diameter) with a woody, ribbed outer texture. Embedded in the pulp within the pods are twenty-five to fifty almond-shaped, whitish, lavender, or purplish seeds about one inch across.

During the harvest season (four-fifths of the world crop is harvested between September and March) the ripened pods are slashed from the tree and broken open with machete knives. Seeds and pulp are removed and left to ferment (three to ten days). During the fermentation period the seeds or beans become plump and moist, and are then easily separated from the pulp, which is discarded. Now the beans are washed, dried, and roasted to 257–350 degrees, after which the shells are removed and the nibs blended into either a solid mass or dark, brown-black liquor. These substances closely resemble what we know as baker's chocolate, or simply unsweetened chocolate. It might also be termed chocolate in the raw, since this form precedes the processing of all the others, including cocoa, milk chocolate, and the varying grades and degrees of sweetened chocolate.

The brief history of chocolate is fairly simple. In pre-Colombian days the beans were used as a medium of exchange by the Mayan and Aztec tribes (maybe some of our real modern-day chocolate lovers would consider some sort of chocolate barter system?). Among his many accomplishments, Christopher Columbus introduced chocolate to Spain as a hot, bitter drink upon his return from South America in 1502. Either the drink was not so good, or the Spanish just wanted to keep it to themselves, since it didn't spread around Europe or to England until over a hundred years later, and even then it achieved only minimal popularity. The British take credit for adding milk to the drink, but it wasn't until the mid-nineteenth century that a process was found to extract the correct proportion of the greasy cocoa butter and create a truly pleasant-tasting substance. Once this had been accomplished, it would seem that everyone jumped on the production bandwagon, and chocolate began its uphill climb toward the incredible popularity it has achieved today.

Ever wonder how they get all those neat little chips so evenly distributed in ice creams such as Chocolate Chip, Chocolate Mint, or Chopped Chocolate? The ice cream mixture, be it vanilla, milk chocolate, or mint-flavored base, is pumped in semisoft form from the mixing vat through a pipe to a smaller holding container. As it passes through this container, it is given a blast of molten semi-sweet chocolate. The interaction of the freezing ice cream mixture with the warm liquid chocolate causes a shattering effect—thus, neat little chocolate chips and all those great flavors.

Following are more chocolate recipes than the greatest chocolate fanatic could possibly handle.

CREME DE CHOCOLAT AU RHUM

4 tablespoons rum or brandy
1 teaspoon Curaçao or other orange liqueur
2 teaspoons creme de cacao, optional

2 teaspoons instant coffee
1 pint Baskin-Robbins Chocolate Fudge Ice Cream, slightly softened

Dissolve instant coffee in rum, Curaçao, and creme de cacao in a blender jar or bowl. Add ice cream and blend just to a thick consistency. Makes 2 servings.

William Maher, St. Louis, Missouri (1975)

CHOCOLATE LOVERS' PIE

1⅓ cups chocolate-wafer crumbs	1 pint Baskin-Robbins Bavarian Chocolate Mint Ice Cream
1 quart Baskin-Robbins Chocolate Fudge Ice Cream	3 tablespoons soft butter

Mix crumbs and butter until crumbly. Press to bottom and sides of 9-inch pie pan. Bake at 375 degrees for 8 minutes. Cool; chill. Spread slightly softened Chocolate Fudge Ice Cream over crust, mounding in center. Spread layer slightly softened Bavarian Ice Cream over Chocolate Fudge, texturing surface with spoon. Freeze 2 or more hours. Makes 10 generous servings.

CHOCOLATE ALMOND TORTE

No special molds are needed for a spectacular-looking torte. Simply fill round cake pans with slightly softened ice creams. Freeze until firm, unmold, stack the layers of ice cream, and frost.

1 quart Baskin-Robbins Chocolate Almond Ice Cream	1 pint whipping cream
	¼ cup sugar
	1 cup sliced, toasted almonds
1 quart Baskin-Robbins Jamoca® Almond Fudge Ice Cream	10 maraschino cherries, halved
2 teaspoons chocolate extract	2 ten-cent chocolate bars, optional

(The torte can be made in 4 layers by filling each pan with one layer of each ice cream.) Line two 8-inch round cake pans with waxed paper. Slightly soften the Chocolate Almond Ice Cream; fill one pan (level with top) with ice cream. Freeze at least 1 hour. Fill second pan with Jamoca® Almond Fudge. Freeze. Place plate on which torte is to be served in refrigerator. Beat cream and chocolate extract until it begins to thicken; gradually add sugar, beating cream until it holds its shape. Remove ice cream from the two pans; peel off waxed paper. Put Chocolate Almond layer on chilled serving plate; spread top lightly with chocolate whipped cream. Top with second ice cream layer; press into place.

Working quickly, frost sides of torte with part of the chocolate whipped cream. Freeze for 30 minutes. Remove from freezer; with fingers or a teaspoon, press sliced almonds into sides of torte. Frost and swirl top with whipped cream. Garnish with cherries. (If desired, chocolate bars can be cut in strips and pressed sideways into top of torte.) Freeze at least 2 hours. Let mellow in refrigerator for 10 minutes before cutting into wedges. Makes 10 to 12 servings.

Carolyn Sweet, Maxwell, California (1973)

CHOCOLATE RUM SUNDAE

2 squares (1 ounce each) semisweet chocolate	1 tablespoon grated orange peel
½ cup firmly packed brown sugar	1 quart Baskin-Robbins Burgundy Cherry or Chocolate Almond Ice Cream
⅓ cup half 'n half cream Pinch of salt	
2 tablespoons rum	

Place chocolate, sugar, cream, and salt in saucepan. Cook, stirring, over low heat until chocolate is melted and smooth, about 2 to 3 minutes. Remove from heat; stir in grated peel and rum. Cool. (Sauce keeps well in refrigerator.) Spoon over scoops of ice cream. Makes 6 to 8 servings.

Lois Bee Martin Doyle, Salem, Virginia (1975)

DOUBLE CHOCOLATE CREPES

1 ounce unsweetened chocolate	¾ cup all-purpose flour
2 eggs	1½ cups Chocolate Sauce (recipe below)
¼ cup sugar	1 quart Baskin-Robbins
1 teaspoon salt	Chocolate Almond
¼ teaspoon cinnamon	or French Vanilla
1 cup water	Ice Cream
½ cup light cream	Chopped walnuts, optional

Melt chocolate over hot water. Beat eggs until thick and light yellow. Slowly add sugar and salt to eggs, beating well after each addition. Stir in chocolate and cinnamon. Combine water and cream and add alternately with flour to chocolate mixture. To make crepes, pour about 2 tablespoons of batter onto a hot, greased griddle. Swirl batter out to make a thin crepe; cook and turn once to brown other side.

194

Store crepes between pieces of waxed paper until ready to use. Makes 12 to 14 crepes.

To make Chocolate Sauce: Melt 1 cup semisweet chocolate bits and ½ ounce unsweetened chocolate over hot water. Stir in ½ cup dairy sour cream, ¼ teaspoon cinnamon, and ¼ cup milk. Blend well. Serve warm.

To serve: Working quickly, spread a scoop of ice cream across the bottom edge of each crepe; roll tightly. Place filled crepes in freezer just until all are made. Place two filled crepes on each desert plate; top with warm chocolate sauce, and, if desired, chopped nuts. Serve immediately. Makes 6 to 7 servings.

Linda J. Claff, Belmont, Massachusetts (1973)

BROWNIE MINT SANDWICH SQUARES

1 recipe brownies, baked, cooled, chilled
2 quarts Baskin-Robbins Chocolate Mint Ice Cream
¼ cup semisweet chocolate pieces
2 tablespoons margarine
½ cup butter
¼ teaspoon salt
1 teaspoon mint flavoring
1 pound confectioners' sugar
4 to 5 tablespoons milk
Green food coloring

Use 22-ounce package walnut brownies, baked in 13″ × 9″ × 2″ pan. Remove chilled brownies from pan and cut in two lengthwise layers. Return bottom layer to pan and spread with slightly softened ice cream; cover with top layer of brownies. Freeze while making frosting. Melt chocolate bits and margarine in small skillet; keep warm. With electric mixer blend butter, salt, and flavoring with a part of the confectioners' sugar until creamy. Add remaining sugar and milk alternately; beat until smooth and creamy. Add food coloring until desired color is reached. Frost top of brownies with this mixture; drizzle with melted chocolate mixture. Cut in large squares and serve; or freeze until needed. Makes 12 to 18 servings.

Carolyn Reynolds, Tacoma, Washington (1973)

MONTEZUMA DELIGHT

Gently heat 1 cup fudge sauce and 1 teaspoon instant coffee. Spoon over large scoops of Peppermint Fudge Ribbon Ice Cream. Sprinkle with slivered almonds.

ACAPULCO FLIP

Place 3 large scoops of Chocolate or Chocolate Fudge Ice Cream and ½ cup of Kahlua or coffee liqueur in blender. Blend just until smooth.

CHOCOLATE-MINT SODA

In tall glass put 2 scoops of Bavarian Chocolate Mint Ice Cream; add ½ cup cold milk. Fill glass with chilled club soda. Stir gently.

DOUBLE CHOCOLATE SODA

For each soda, put 2 or 3 tablespoons of chocolate syrup in tall glass. Fill glass half full with chilled club soda. Add two generous scoops of Bavarian Chocolate Mint Ice Cream. Thread large marshmallow and red maraschino cherry on a striped straw. Serve in glass.

HOT FUDGE SAUCE

2 squares (2 ounces) un- sweetened chocolate	⅔ cup evaporated milk 1 tablespoon butter
1 cup sugar	1 teaspoon vanilla

Combine first 3 ingredients in top of double boiler. Cook over simmering water, stirring occasionally, about 30 minutes, until sauce thickens and becomes glossy and smooth. Stir in butter and vanilla. Remove from heat, but let sauce stand over hot water until needed. To store spoon into jar and refrigerate. To reheat, set jar in a pan of warm water; bring water just to a simmer over medium heat. Makes 1½ cups hot fudge sauce.

CANDY BAR PIE

This dessert has three different fudge flavors in one recipe.

3 tablespoons soft butter or
  margarine
	1 quart Baskin-Robbins
	  Coconut Almond

2 cups flaked coconut	Fudge Ice Cream

1 quart Baskin-Robbins
  Chocolate Fudge Ice
  Cream
	1 recipe Hot Fudge Sauce
	  (optional)

Spread butter on bottom and sides of a 9-inch pie pan. With fingers, press coconut evenly and firmly against buttered areas. Bake in a preheated 300-degree oven for 15 minutes, or until golden brown. Cool. Freeze at least 2 hours. Slightly soften the Chocolate Fudge Ice Cream; smooth into frozen shell, mounding center. Top with scoops of Coconut Almond Fudge Ice Cream. Freeze at least 3 hours. At serving time cut into wedges, and if desired, drizzle each serving with warm fudge sauce. Makes 8 to 10 servings.

OCTOBER

While October can and does offer some of the most beautiful sunsets, the pleasantest temperatures, and most spectacular colors of the year, it also carries a connotation of the approaching death of the old year. In areas where climatic changes are most severe, it is almost as if the colors of October are one last defiant binge on the part of nature before everything is again blanketed with the bleakness of winter.

This writer had the good fortune during several Octobers to be part of the cranberry harvest in the marshy bogs on the Massachusetts south shore. The days were sunny but the air sharp, and the vivid picture of the waxy red berries being boxed against a background of flame red and orange leaves is one never to be forgotten. The sky was a brighter blue than the sky of August or September, and there was always the threat of frost at night, and then the bogs would have to be flooded. Later on in the season flooded bogs meant great ice skating.

October culminates with Hallowe'en, the ultimate festival of night which epitomizes the surreal climate of the month itself. In many other countries and certain regions of our own there are harvest festivals, such as Oktoberfest in Germany. Our major harvest event comes later in November in the form of Thanksgiving, but it is actually long before the third week in November that the harvest has been accomplished. Thanksgiving Day was originally proclaimed on October 3, 1789. October is harvest month.

But when you grow tired of all that pumpkin and butternut squash, there is still a year-round treat called ice cream, and we offer you a number of exotic and delicious frozen confections to assist you in celebrating the beauty of October.

Libra

Of all the recipes available to us, this unusual popcorn basket seemed most appropriate for Li-

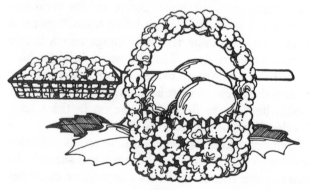

brans. If they can't think of anything else to do with it, at least they can hang it up and achieve their much-sought-after balance.

PARTY POPCORN BASKETS

1 pan (5 ounces) pop-at-home popcorn or 10 cups popped corn
1 cup sugar
½ cup corn syrup
½ cup water
¼ cup butter or margarine
Small bowls, holding about 10 to 12 ounces, 4″ to 5″ diameter
Paper baking cups

1 pint Baskin-Robbins Burgundy Cherry Ice Cream
1 pint Baskin-Robbins Banana Marshmallow Ice Cream
1 pint Baskin-Robbins Fresh Strawberry Ice Cream
Gumdrops, licorice whips, optional

Prepare popcorn according to package directions. Cool. Combine sugar, corn syrup, and water in a saucepan; boil until mixture reaches 240 degrees on a candy thermometer (or until mixture dropped from a spoon into cold water forms a soft ball). Remove from heat; stir in butter. Place popped corn in a large bowl. Pour hot syrup over and mix thoroughly. Let cool until slightly sticky and workable. Mold inside buttered bowls to form 6 basket shapes. (If desired, form "handles" over top of buttered custard cups.) Refrigerate briefly to harden. Remove popcorn baskets from bowls and wrap carefully in plastic wrap. Scoop 6 small balls of each flavor ice cream. Place 1 scoop of each flavor in 6 paper baking cups (3 scoops per cup). Freeze until needed. At serving time, place a cup in each basket. If desired, decorate with gumdrops and licorice whips. Place handle atop basket. Makes 6 servings.

Vivian Friend, Staten Island, New York (1975)

Columbus Day Drinks

Italy's Galliano has become one of America's most popular liqueurs, second only perhaps to Mexico's Kahlua. The Galliano Screwdriver (Harvey Wollbanger) has done a great deal to promote the liqueur. Why not try a Harvey Wollbanger float? Make your usual drink with orange juice, vodka and Galliano, then float a scoop of Baskin-Robbins Orange Sherbet or French Vanilla on top. In honor of that most famous Italian who made us all possible by discovering this continent, we present the two following drinks, both different and delicious. Christopher Columbus, you're on!

CHOC-LIANO MINT

1 quart Baskin-Robbins Chocolate Fudge Ice Cream	⅓ cup Liqueur Galliano
	⅓ cup creme de menthe
	Dash of nutmeg

In blender or a large bowl, mix ice cream, Galliano, and creme de menthe just until smooth. Pour into 4 glasses; sprinkle lightly with nutmeg. Makes 4 servings.

Edward K. Kuzdal, Three Oaks, Michigan (1973)

FROZEN CAPPUCCINO

1 quart Baskin-Robbins ¼ cup milk
  Jamoca® Almond ⅓ cup brandy, or more
  Fudge Ice Cream

Pour the milk and brandy into the blender container. Add 6 scoops of slightly softened Jamoca® Almond Fudge Ice Cream. Whir just until blended; pour into stemmed glasses. Top, if desired, with chocolate curls. Makes 4 to 5 servings.

Irv, the Pied Piper

People have even gone as far as to regard **Irv** Robbins as a sort of Pied Piper. And he loves it. One October night in Encino, he was sauntering along Ventura Boulevard and a young couple pulled alongside and said, "You wouldn't know where there's a Baskin-Robbins?" Delighted, Irv pointed them in the right direction, not revealing his identity. The couple happily sped off toward their waiting treats.

When he got in his car and looked at the clock, Irv realized it was after closing time and the couple would have to go ice-cream-less that night (unless, horror of horrors, they managed to find a Swenson's or Wil Wright's open at such a late hour—or, worse still, they would succumb to the questionable temptation of supermarket ice cream). Seeking to protect his new friends from a fate worse than ketchup ice cream, Irv gave chase and caught up with the couple just as they were solemnly pulling away from the darkened store. A little startled, they finally recognized the friendly face beckoning at them from the little brown sports car and accepted a jovial invitation from this total stranger to "Come and have some ice cream with me." If they hadn't yet realized his identity, they must have gotten a laugh when they began to follow him and saw the California "vanity" plate, "BR 31." When they reached the Robbins home they were taken immediately to the unique basement soda fountain (modeled exactly after a Baskin-Robbins store) and offered their choice of 31 flavors, sumptuous sundaes, and sodas, just as if they'd made it to the Encino store in time.

The license plate has been chased on the freeways

on occasion as well, and one man actually followed Irv all the way from Glendale through several interchanges, off the freeway, and up Victory Boulevard to Baskin-Robbins headquarters. When he emerged from his car and spoke to Irv, the man said, "I saw the plate and knew if I followed it long enough it would lead me to some of your ice cream." All of us have had the desire to seek the pot of gold at the end of the rainbow, but usually the reward is not so concrete or immediate. This man, a busy publisher, took valuable time from his day to search for the perfect ice cream cone. When a freak's on the search, there's no holding him back!

MARGARITA PIE

When the nights begin to grow colder, spice them up with a red-hot Mexican dinner, followed by a tangy Margarita Pie.

Pretzel Crumb Crust: Mix ¾ cup finely crushed pretzel crumbs with 3 tablespoons sugar. Gradually add 5 tablespoons melted butter. Mix well. Reserve 2 tablespoons pretzel crumbs. Press remaining mixture into bottom and sides of well-buttered 9-inch pie plate. Chill.

Filling: Stir about ¼ cup Tequila and 2 tablespoons Triple Sec into softened Lemon Custard Ice Cream (at least one quart). Fill pretzel crust with mixture. Garnish with reserved pretzel crumbs and freeze at least 5 hours before serving.

With Employees Like This, Who Needs an Ad Agency?

Baskin-Robbins employees are loyal to the death. One of the most devoted had surgery several years ago, and on her way out of the operating room vaguely heard the nurse say to the doctor, "Gee, I'm hungry. Let's order a milkshake and sandwiches." While it is generally against policy for hospital employees to divulge what a patient has uttered under sedation, the recovery room nurse couldn't resist telling the Baskin-Robbins devotee of her groggy suggestion that the doctor and nurse run across the street to Baskin-Robbins and bring her back a double-thick Jamoca® shake.

DATE CHOCOLATE SHAKE

1½ cups cold milk
6 dates, pitted and chopped
2 tablespoons chocolate syrup
Mint sprigs

1 pint Baskin-Robbins Coconut Chocolate Chip or Coconut Almond Fudge Ice Cream

Combine first 3 ingredients in blender. Blend until dates are finely chopped. Add scoops of ice cream and whirl just until blended. Pour into tall glasses and top each with fresh mint. Serves 3 to 4.

Helen Vassallo, Troy, Michigan (1975)

Hallowe'en

Ice cream, even we'll admit, isn't the best trick or treat item, but here are a few party goodies for kids' indoor activities on Hallowe'en (and there's one for adults, too).

ORANGE JACK-O-LANTERNS

Cut off the top of fresh orange and scoop out pulp, leaving the shell intact. Notch-cut edge of shell and cut a jack-o-lantern face in shell if desired. Fill with Orange Sherbet or Licorice Ice Cream. Freeze till needed. Same procedure for tangerines, as well as fresh pumpkins for a Hallowe'en party treat!

• • •

Can you imagine going to a Hallowe'en party as a hot fudge sundae? One BR fan (and we assume his mother or dad) spent several weeks dreaming up a pink and brown polka-dotted cup suit. His chest appropriately was attired as the ice cream, fudge sauce, and whipped cream, and of course, his head was the cherry. He won the prize at his party . . . a free hot fudge sundae at Howard Johnson's!

• • •

GRANOLA GOODIES

For each serving: take one generous scoop Baskin-Robbins Chocolate Chip Ice Cream; pour ¼ cup of your favorite Granola into a good-sized square of waxed paper. Roll the ice cream in the Granola, form into a ball, insert a wooden popsicle stick, and freeze. Great Hallowe'en party treats.

While the kids are eating their Granola goodies, parents can indulge in the spirit of Hallowe'en with this incredible hot buttered rum. Once you've tried it, don't restrict your indulgence to this one day. It's always ready in your freezer, and it is delicious!

EVER-READY HOT BUTTERED RUM

Make this rich batter ahead of time, store in the freezer, and be ready to serve hot buttered rum spontaneously.

1 quart Baskin-Robbins French Vanilla Ice Cream	1 pound brown sugar
	2 teaspoons nutmeg
	2 teaspoons cinnamon
1 pound butter	Rum
1 pound confectioners' sugar	Cinnamon sticks, optional
	Boiling water

In a large bowl let ice cream and butter sit at room temperature until soft. Mix together; stir in sugars, nutmeg, and cinnamon. Blend until smooth. Freeze. (Mixture remains spoonable.) To serve, spoon 3 tablespoons batter in mug; add 1 jigger of rum and 6 ounces of boiling water. (Or use boiling cider and 2 tablespoons of batter.) If desired, use cinnamon sticks as stirrers. Makes about 30 servings.

Anne S. Mather, Houston, Texas (1973)

NOVEMBER

Poor old November, it has its moments, even if it does seem to signal the beginning of winter. Things slow down early in the month (a calm before the holiday storms to come?) and this is the time of year when snow once again seems ethereal and romantic ... not depressing and never-ending as it does in March.

The first snowfall in our snowier regions can come earlier than November, but generally it sneaks in sometime just before Thanksgiving. The true mystery of snow lies in its silence: all that matter falling and accumulating, causing both joy and anxiety. In the east a decent snowfall always meant the possibility of school cancellation: two long blasts of the local fire station horn at 8 A.M. meant the day was free. For the young kids it meant sledding and snowball fights; for the more enterprising older ones it meant some pocket money from shoveling driveways and walks.

Ice cream is a great pacifier for bored kids shut inside on the first rainy or snowy days. There are some simple kids' recipes here that are just perfect as a break from a day-long game of Monopoly or a never-ending bout with a model ship or airplane.

Thanksgiving dominates the flavor of this month, although it comes near the end and nearly everywhere now the commercial trappings of Christmas-to-come rule over both the landscape and airwaves. Thanksgiving does begin the round of festive events that won't stop until that magical ball drops from the Time/Life Building in New York January 1. So November should be thought of as anything but dreary—it's just the beginning of a season of the year when people are encouraged to open their hearts to each other and celebrate the miracle that another year has passed—and, better still—another one is coming. Maybe we should start a movement to change the name to Yesvember?

Scorpio

Here is a spirited ice cream drink that's reminiscent of a Stinger. It has, in addition to rum and brandy, some almond syrup, orange and lemon juice, and Baskin-Robbins Lemon Custard Ice Cream. Offer it to your favorite Scorpio as a birthday treat—it'll give 'em a sting back!

SCORPION FLOAT

1½ cups orange juice
2 teaspoons lemon juice
1 tablespoon orgeat (almond syrup)
Fresh orange sections

2 tablespoons rum
1 pint Baskin-Robbins Lemon Custard Ice Cream
2 tablespoons brandy

Mix orange juice, lemon juice, orgeat, brandy, and rum. Place 2 scoops of ice cream into 2 or 3 tall glasses. Pour mixture over ice cream. Garnish, if desired, with orange sections. Makes 2 to 3 servings.

Segrid Ann Ellis, Greensboro, North Carolina
(1975)

Kids' Days

Here are three simple ice cream goodies kids will welcome on those first "inside" days during November. Ice cream is the best kid-pleaser there is.

MIGHTY GORILLA

Strictly for kids—no spoons, please. Spoon ½ cup peanut butter into a small skillet and heat over low heat until soft and creamy. From a quart of Baskin-Robbins Jamoca® Ice Cream scoop 2 scoops of ice cream into each of 4 serving dishes; top with peanut butter. Take 12 pretzel rods (6″ long, ½″ diameter) and insert 3 pretzel rods, at an angle, into each serving of ice cream. (Use the rods, instead of spoons, to eat the ice cream!) Makes 4 large servings.

Barbara Wilkerson, Bethesda, Maryland (1973)

LEMON CUSTARD ICE CREAM SODA

From a pint of Baskin-Robbins Lemon Custard Ice Cream, place two scoops in each of two tall glasses. In blender, put 2 tablespoons orange marmalade, ½ cup milk, 1 cup orange juice, and 2 scoops of ice cream. Blend just until smooth. Pour over ice cream in glasses; top off with chilled ginger ale. Makes 2 servings.

Eva M. Ware, Woodland Park, Colorado (1973)

PURPLE PASSION PARFAITS

Cut 1 large, ripe banana in two crosswise. Peel one half; set other half aside. Mash the peeled half banana; mix in one 6-ounce can frozen grape juice concentrate. From a quart of Baskin-Robbins Burgundy Cherry (or Vanilla) Ice Cream place scoops in bottom of each of 6 parfait glasses. Alternate layers of banana-grape juice mixture and ice cream until glasses are filled. Freeze. To serve, top each parfait with slices from the remaining half banana. Makes 6 servings.

Lynn Thiel, Oshkosh, Wisconsin (1973)

Election Day

Back in the days when politics involved a sense of humor, Baskin and Robbins devised a flavor they called Candi-Date for the 1960 Presidential election. They thought it would be fun to print up a few colorful signs and sell just this flavor during the Democratic National Convention at the L.A. Sports Arena. But Robbins got involved in his own politics when he approached the concessionaire, who nixed the whole project. Enterprising Irv thought Candi-Date was too good a thing to give up without a

217

fight, so he offered the guy a healthy percentage—fifty percent of all sales. After a few minutes the discussion ended, and Irv got his way: the ice cream would be sold during the Convention, but only with Irv supplying it free to the concessionaire, who then took a hundred percent profit. Maybe politics doesn't pay after all.

Veteran's Day

In honor of Veteran's Day (or Armistice Day, as it used to be called), November 11, or whatever day they've made it now that legislation has standardized holidays, here is a simple dessert, submitted to the 1973 Show Off by Major Martin Ischinger of the U.S. Army Academy at West Point. According to the Major, this dessert is a favorite of West Point cadets: bowls of honey, peanut butter, and butter are placed on each long table, and the cadets make up their own Sammy Sauce, which they then spoon onto their ice cream. One gets the feeling that the Army wouldn't actually be supplying Baskin-Robbins ice cream, but it's the thought that counts, Major Ischinger!

WEST POINT SAMMY

Blend ½ cup pure honey, ⅓ cup peanut butter, and 3 tablespoons soft butter together until smooth.

218

Spoon over 3 scoops of Baskin-Robbins French Vanilla Ice Cream. Makes 1 generous serving.

Major Martin Ischinger, West Point, New York (1973)

First Snowfall

Welcome the first snowfall with your own snowball, a great combination of marshmallow, coconut, and chocolate.

SAUCY SNOWBALL

1 quart Baskin-Robbins Fresh Coconut Ice Cream
1 cup flaked coconut
1 can (14 ounces) sweetened condensed milk
½ cup milk
1 package (12 ounces) semisweet chocolate bits
1 jar (7 ounces) marshmallow creme
1 teaspoon vanilla
8 red birthday candles

Roll scoops of Fresh Coconut Ice Cream in the flaked coconut. Freeze. Combine the remaining ingredients (except the candles!) in a saucepan. Heat over medium heat, stirring, just until mixture is smooth and warmed through. (If desired, the sauce can be refrigerated and reheated just before serving.) At serving time, ladle the warm sauce into a stemmed compote or sherbet dish, top with a frozen snowball, and insert a red candle. Makes 8 to 10 servings.

Thanksgiving

Thanksgiving, maybe more than any other American holiday, is a time when people want to outdo themselves in the kitchen to please the people they love. So why try to do it with the same old standbys? Sure, plain pumpkin or mince pie and plum pudding have their merits, but their charm fades a bit after the twentieth year or so. Ice cream is a great variant for Thanksgiving desserts and other treats, and you'll find that peoples' palates willingly accept the cool, refreshing texture of ice cream after a rich, filling repast.

But don't avoid pumpkin pie just to be different! You can serve the richest, most elegant, and easy-to-prepare pumpkin pie ever and be as different as if you'd served the most complicated chilled soufflé. This pumpkin pie has Baskin-Robbins Butter Pecan Ice Cream as its crust, and once you've tasted it you'll never look on plain old pumpkin pie quite the same. It's a treat worthy of anyone's thanks.

PUMPKIN PECAN PARTY PIE

1½ quarts Baskin-Robbins Butter Pecan Ice Cream
1 cup sugar
1 cup canned pumpkin
1 teaspoon cinnamon
¼ teaspoon *each* ginger, nutmeg, salt
1 cup whipping cream, whipped
¼ cup packed light brown sugar
2 tablespoons butter
1 tablespoon water
½ cup chopped pecans

(Thirty minutes before preparing ice cream crust, put a deep 9-inch pie pan in freezer.) To make crust: working quickly, line bottom and sides of frozen pan with ice cream. Do not put ice cream on edge of pan. Build up crust ½ inch above edge of pan by overlapping tablespoonfuls of ice cream. Freeze at least 2 hours. Combine sugar, pumpkin, spices, and salt in a saucepan; cook over low heat for 3 minutes. Cool. Reserve ¼ cup whipped cream for garnish. Fold remaining whipped cream into pumpkin mixture. Spoon into frozen ice cream crust, swirling top. Freeze at least 2 hours. In small saucepan over medium heat, combine brown sugar, butter, and water. Bring just to a boil, cook 1½ minutes, remove from heat, stir in pecans. Cool. Spoon mixture around edge between filling and crust. Mound the ¼ cup of reserved whipped cream in center. Freeze. Let mellow for 10 minutes in refrigerator; cut in wedges. Makes 8 to 10 servings.

Susan T. Burtch, Richmond, Virginia (1973)

Pumpkin pie isn't the only trick we're holding for your Thanksgiving table. Here's another pie that's just as festive, just light enough to follow a sumptuous meal.

RUM NOG PIE

1 quart Baskin-Robbins
    Jamoca® Ice Cream
½ cup light rum
Chocolate curls, or toasted
    walnuts

1 pint Baskin-Robbins
    Egg Nog Ice Cream
12 chocolate wafers

Toast walnuts ahead of time. Spread chopped California walnuts, in a single layer, in a shallow pan; bake 10 minutes in a preheated 375-degree oven. Cool. Thirty minutes before making pie, put a deep 9-inch pie pan and a 2-quart bowl in the freezer. Scoop the Jamoca® Ice Cream into the chilled bowl; let stand *just until slightly mellowed.* Stir in the rum. Spread the Jamoca® Ice Cream in the bottom of the frozen pie pan. Freeze 3 hours. Using an ice cream spade cover the bottom ice cream layer with overlapping slices of Egg Nog Ice Cream. Press the chocolate wafers around the edge of the pie. Top with chocolate curls or toasted walnuts. Freeze 2 hours. Makes 6 to 8 servings.

Here's another super colorful, multi-flavored rum pie variation.

222

AUNT MARY'S RUM RUNNER PIE

1½ cups graham crackers
    (about 15 crackers)
4 tablespoons sugar
½ cup butter, melted
¾ cup apricot jam
2 tablespoons rum or
    brandy
1 quart Baskin-Robbins
    Lemon Custard Ice
    Cream

1 pint Baskin-Robbins
    Fresh Coconut Ice
    Cream
4 canned cling peach
    halves, drained
3 canned pineapple
    slices, halved,
    drained
5 maraschino cherries,
    halved

Blend crumbs, sugar, and butter; press into bottom and sides of a 9- or 10-inch pie pan. Freeze. Melt jam in a heavy saucepan over medium heat; when bubbling add rum and cook for 2 minutes. Remove from heat and press through a fine sieve. Cool. Slightly soften the Lemon Custard Ice Cream and spoon into crust, gently pressing it into a level layer. Freeze for 1 hour. Top with about two-thirds of the Coconut Ice Cream, pressing it into a layer. (Or use other Baskin-Robbins lemon- and coconut-flavored ice creams.) Arrange half slices of pineapple around edge of pie to form a scalloped edge. Place one peach half, cut side up, in center of pie, arrange remaining halves around center peach, cut sides up. Place a half cherry, cut side down, in the center of each peach half. Cover top of pie with apricot glaze. Freeze for at least 3 hours. Makes 8 to 10 servings.

Diana Stanfield, Santa Monica, California (1973)

223

For those who can't resist rushing the eggnog season a bit, here's a dessert compromise: a rich, creamy sundae. Another super Thanksgiving Day dessert.

DUTCH EGGNOG DELIGHT

10 eggs
1¼ cups sugar
¼ teaspoon salt
Pinch of nutmeg
Whipped cream, optional
2 cups brandy

1½ teaspoons vanilla
2 quarts Baskin-Robbins
Chocolate Fudge or
French Vanilla Ice
Cream

Beat eggs with sugar, salt, and nutmeg until very thick. Slowly add the brandy, beating constantly. Pour mixture into a heavy saucepan or double boiler. Cook over very low heat, beating constantly, until eggnog is warm (not hot) and thickened. Remove from heat; stir in vanilla. Cool. Refrigerate. At serving time put one scoop of ice cream in each sherbet or champagne glass. Pour eggnog, warm or cold, over ice cream and, if desired, top each with a dollop of whipped cream. Makes 16 servings.

Hendrica Elia, Memphis, Tennessee (1975)

Who ever thought of taking the jellied cranberry sauce and whipping it up into a Thanksgiving punch? A Baskin-Robbins fan, naturally. This is a great holiday punch for kids and adults.

THANKSGIVING PUNCH

1 pint Baskin-Robbins Burgundy Cherry Ice Cream
1 can (8 ounces) jellied cranberry sauce
1 can (12 ounces) diet cream soda

1 unpeeled orange, thinly sliced
½ cup drained, pitted dark sweet cherries, optional

Mix ice cream with cranberry sauce just until smooth. Divide mixture into 4 glasses. Fill glasses with soda. Garnish glasses with orange slices; add cherries if desired. Makes 4 servings.

Karolyn Knepler, Santa Maria, California (1975)

Spicy gingersnaps and creamy Lemon Custard Ice Cream combine for a really different dessert that's light enough to follow the most sumptuous Thanksgiving dinner.

LEMON CUSTARD MERINGUE PIE

1½ cups fine gingersnap crumbs	2 egg whites
⅓ cup melted butter	¼ cup water
1 quart Baskin-Robbins Lemon Custard Ice Cream	1 cup sugar
	1½ tablespoons molasses
	⅛ teaspoon salt
	½ teaspoon vanilla extract

Blend crumbs and butter; press into bottom and sides of a 10-inch pie pan. Bake in a preheated 350-degree oven for 10 minutes. Chill. Slightly soften Lemon Custard Ice Cream, or any other Baskin-Robbins lemon-flavored ice cream, and spoon into chilled crust, gently pressing it into a layer. Cover with foil; freeze for at least 2 hours. Then, combine egg whites, water, sugar, molasses, and salt in top of double boiler. Beat over boiling water with rotary or electric mixer until meringue stands in peaks, about 7 minutes. Remove from heat, stir in vanilla, beat or cool slightly, about 2 minutes. Cover and refrigerate. Just before serving, take pie from freezer, remove foil, spread meringue in a swirl over top of ice cream. Cut in wedges to serve. Makes 6 to 8 servings.

Connie Schwartzman, Rolling Hills, California (1973)

DECEMBER

In addition to being the calendar year's most festive month, December is Baskin-Robbins' birthday month. It was on December 7, 1945 that Irv Robbins opened the doors on his first Snowbird store in Glendale, California. It just happens that the year this book is published is also the eve of Baskin-Robbins' 31st Birthday—the birth date in 1975 marks the first day of the company's 31st year. Thirty-one years of thirty-one flavors. It also happens that this momentous, once-in-a-lifetime event concurs with the 200th birthday of the United States of America—so everybody will be inadvertently helping to celebrate Baskin-Robbins' big year all year long.

Let's all begin the celebration in grand style by using ice cream in as many ways as possible throughout the month. December's festive occasions call for more unique and creative menu and party planning than any other time during the year, so be sure to use ice cream to make your job easier and more fun. Most people end up going to function after function, eating the same old standard things, and it can get pretty dull after a while—standard egg nog, pumpkin and mince pies, plum puddings, turkey and ham. Nobody likes a dull party, a dull meal, or a dull dessert, so get with it this December and pick out and serve some of the great recipes included here.

Sagittarius

SAGITTARIUS NOG

Here's a holiday drink that's spicy and spirited enough for fiery, clownish Sagittarius. Combining chocolate, Kahlua, and the unusual flavor of Galliano, it's more than mocha.

1 pint Baskin-Robbins Chocolate Fudge Ice Cream	1 ice cube, finely crushed
	¼ cup light cream
	Cinnamon
⅓ cup Liquore Galliano	
¼ cup Kahlua	

Scoop ice cream into blender; add remaining ingredients except cinnamon. Blend on high speed just until smooth. Pour into 4 Irish coffee mugs or stemmed glasses. Sprinkle with cinnamon. Makes 4 servings.

Selma Albrecht, Minneapolis, Minnesota (1973)

If That's a "31" Can This Be Belgium?

On December 7, 1947, precisely twenty-nine years from the date that Irv Robbins first hung out the sign on his Snowbird store, Baskin-Robbins opened their first store in Europe just outside of Brussels. The opening was the result of an intense research and development program, and the store and four other subsequent Belgian outlets have proved tremendously successful. Plans are underway for additional European expansion.

The Belgian stores, in addition to the Japanese ones, staged their own Ice Cream Show Off in 1975. Entries were given a preliminary judging at the Brussels headquarters of BR Europe and the winners sent on to Burbank, where they were tested and given a final judging. Following is the Grand Prize Belgian winner, a simple but delicious combination of ice cream and hot pudding—great for kids on a cold, late fall day.

HOT JAMOCA® BUTTERSCOTCH PARFAIT

Six-ounce package cooked butterscotch pudding mix

1 pint Baskin-Robbins Jamoca® Ice Cream
Whipped cream (optional)

Prepare pudding mix according to package instructions. In tall parfait glasses alternate layers of hot butterscotch pudding with Jamoca® Ice Cream. Top with whipped cream. Makes 6 generous servings.

Maxine Carr, Overijse, Belgium (1975)

Baskin-Robbins' Birthday

All loyal Baskin-Robbins fans will begin the celebration of "Thirty-One-derful Years" by going to their local store and buying some of the "Thirty-One-derful" flavors. Once you've bought them, take them home and have a party, and treat yourselves to one, some, or all of the following goodies.

BR BIRTHDAY BOMBE

1 package (18½ ounces) chocolate cake mix
1 teaspoon brandy extract
1 pint Baskin-Robbins Chocolate Mint Ice Cream
1 pint Baskin-Robbins Fresh Coconut Ice Cream*

1 pint Baskin-Robbins Burgundy Cherry Ice Cream
1 teaspoon chocolate extract
1 jar (9 ounces) Baskin-Robbins Hot Fudge
¼ cup Grand Marnier Liqueur

Prepare cake mix according to package directions using chocolate extract and brandy extract for flavoring. Pour batter into a greased 2½ quart ovenproof bowl. Bake in a 325-degree preheated oven about 60 minutes, or until cake tester comes out dry about 2 inches in from edge of bowl. Do not remove

* If a Baskin-Robbins coconut-flavored ice cream is not available, use French Vanilla.

cake from bowl. Cool. Scoop out center of cake, leaving a 1½ inch shell. Carefully loosen shell from bowl, but leave in bowl. (Reserve scooped-out cake.*) Soften Chocolate Mint Ice Cream; fill shell one-third full. Repeat with other 2 flavors. Wrap bowl with heavy foil. Freeze at least 3 hours. Place plate on which bombe is to be served in refrigerator. Gently heat fudge sauce, stir in Grand Mariner, remove from heat and cool slightly. Remove bombe from freezer; carefully loosen from bowl with spatula and invert onto chilled serving plate. Pour sauce over bombe. Freeze at least 1 hour. Let mellow in refrigerator 10 minutes before serving. Cut in wedges. Makes 8 to 10 servings.

Marie S. Rattner, Chappaqua, New York (1973)

* Line cupcake pans with paper cups, fill half full with softened Baskin-Robbins ice cream, press broken pieces of cake into ice cream; cover with ice cream, top with ice cream, top with chopped nuts, or sauce. Cover with foil, freeze.

KAHLUA MOUSSE

Baskin-Robbins Chocolate	16 marshmallows
Ice Cream (like	1 cup heavy cream
German Chocolate	1½ ounces Kahlua
Cake, etc.)	Chopped nuts for garnish

Melt marshmallows with ⅓ cup cream in top of double boiler until softened, fluffy, and smooth. Stir in 1½ ounces Kahlua and bring to room temperature. Whip additional ⅔ cup cream and fold into mixture. Turn into freezing tray or individual dish and freeze. (May also be made with Alexanders, Grasshoppers, and Velvet Hammer.) Place layer of BR Chocolate Ice Cream in serving dish. Freeze. Top with layer of mousse. Freeze. Garnish with chopped nuts.

JAMOCA® SUNDAE

1 recipe coffee liqueur	Whipped cream or topping,
(recipe below)	optional
1 quart Baskin-Robbins	Whole pecans, optional
Jamoca® Ice Cream	

Two weeks ahead make coffee liqueur by dissolving, in a large saucepan, ½ cup water and ½ cup instant (not freeze-dried) coffee. When dissolved, add 1 pint of light corn syrup and 1 cup sugar. Bring mixture to a boil, stirring constantly. Reduce heat, simmer, stirring until sugar is dissolved, about 2 minutes. Remove from heat; cool. Stir in 3 tablespoons pure vanilla extract (a 1-ounce bottle) and ⅘ quart of vodka. Pour into a large jar or jars. Cover loosely and let age, at room temperature, for two weeks. To serve: Spoon liqueur over scoops of ice cream in sherbet or dessert dishes. Top each serving, if desired, with whipped cream and pecans. Remainder of liqueur can be stored in jars, at room temperature, until used. Makes 6 servings.

Donna La Cour, Colorado Springs, Colorado
(1973)

CLOVE PINEAPPLE SUNDAE

1 quart Baskin-Robbins
  French Vanilla Ice
  Cream
¾ cup pineapple topping

24 (2 packages) clove-fla-
  vored Lifesavers,
  coarsely crushed

Place 2 scoops of ice cream in each of 4 sherbet or dessert dishes. Top each with 3 tablespoons pineapple topping; sprinkle with crushed Lifesavers. Makes 4 servings.

Gail D. Johnson, Champaign, Illinois (1973)

COCONUT LEMON CRUNCH

2 cups graham cracker crumbs (about 20 crackers)
¾ cup packed light brown sugar
1¼ teaspoons cinnamon
1 cup chopped pecans
½ cup butter, melted
2 quarts Baskin-Robbins Lemon Custard Ice Cream
1 recipe Lemon Drop Whipped Cream

Combine first 5 ingredients. Press one-half this mixture into a baking dish, 13″ × 9″ × 2″. Slightly soften Lemon Custard Ice Cream, or use any other Baskin-Robbins lemon-flavored ice cream. Spread one-half of it over crumb mixture. Sprinkle with one-half the remaining mixture; cover with remaining ice cream; sprinkle with rest of mixture. Wrap in foil; freeze for at least 2 hours.

To make Lemon Drop Whipped Cream: Combine 1 cup whipping cream, whipped; 3 tablespoons sugar, 1 teaspoon grated lemon peel, ¾ cup toasted coconut, and 2 tablespoons crushed candy lemon drops. To serve, cut crunch into squares or bars and top with whipped cream mixture. Makes 12 to 15 servings.

Lillian C. Adams, Lexington, Kentucky (1973)

Start off the Christmas season early on Baskin-Robbins' birthday.

MERRYMINT PARFAIT

1 can (14 ounces) sweetened condensed milk
1 package (12 ounces) semisweet chocolate bits
½ cup milk
1 jar (7 ounces) marsh-mallow creme
1 teaspoon vanilla
1 quart Baskin-Robbins Chocolate Mint Ice Cream

Combine the first 5 ingredients in a saucepan. Heat over medium heat, stirring, just until mixture is smooth and warmed through. Chill. Alternate layers of Baskin-Robbins Chocolate Mint Ice Cream and the sauce in parfait glasses. Freeze until ready to serve. Remove from freezer 10 minutes before serving. (Or, make the wonderful sauce and serve over scoops of Chocolate Mint Ice Cream!) Makes 8 to 10 servings.

Winter's Beginning

WINTER WONDERFUL PUNCH

By the time December 21st rolls around and winter begins, you may be plain tired of the old eggnog circuit, so serve this tart, refreshingly different punch—it's fantastic either hot or cold, and it's just the right color for the season.

2 packages (10 ounces)
    frozen raspberries,
    slightly thawed
1 quart cranberry-apple
    juice

Juice of one lemon
1 quart Baskin-Robbins
    Burgundy Cherry Ice
    Cream

Combine berries and fruit juices in a two-quart saucepan. Simmer for 10 minutes. Pour mixture through a fine sieve, pressing to obtain all possible berry pulp. Serve hot or cold, in mugs, each topped with a scoop of ice cream. Makes 10 to 12 servings.
    Wand Selengowski, Warren, Michigan (1973)

Christmas Recipes

When Christmas finally does arrive, any loyal reader will be well armed with different and tasty ways to go using ice cream for drinks, desserts, and little specialties. December is ice cream dessert month! Knock yourselves out.

GRAPE MINCE-MEAT SUNDAE

½ cup Concord grape juice
1 cup prepared mince
   meat
¼ cup chopped pecans
¼ cup finely chopped can-
   died fruits

¼ cup apricot brandy, op-
   tional
1 quart Baskin-Robbins
   Burgundy Cherry or
   Fresh Coconut Ice
   Cream

Combine first 4 ingredients. If desired, stir in brandy. Serve warm or cold over scoops of ice cream. Makes 6 to 8 servings.

Rachel Bone, Euclid, Ohio (1975)

The world's easiest, most delicious egg nog—perfect for Christmas Eve!

GRANDMOTHER ROBBINS' EGG NOG

1 cup milk
1 cup light rum, bourbon,
   or brandy

1 quart Baskin-Robbins
   Egg Nog Ice Cream

Slightly soften ¾ of the ice cream in a bowl; blend in the milk and rum. Pour into punch cups; float a small scoop of remaining ice cream in each cup. Sprinkle with nutmeg. Makes 8 to 10 servings.

Or try this super variation. . . .

MOCHA EGG NOG PUNCH

1 quart chilled strong   ½ cup whipping cream,
  coffee   whipped
1 quart Egg Nog Ice
  Cream

Beat coffee with half of the ice cream. Add remaining ice cream in scoops. Top with whipped cream. Fills 10 to 12 punch cups.

Don't ignore the kids while the adults are busy enjoying their great holiday egg nogs. Here's one just for the youngsters:

Slightly soften one quart of Baskin-Robbins Egg Nog Ice Cream. Drop 2 or 3 small scoops in each glass; fill with chocolate milk. Makes 10 to 12 servings.

HOLIDAY ICE CREAM BOMBE

1 quart Baskin-Robbins   1 recipe Holly Berry Sauce
   Rum Raisin Ice   (optional)
   Cream*
1 quart Baskin-Robbins
   Spumoni Ice Cream*

Slightly soften the Rum Raisin Ice Cream. Spoon into a chilled 2-quart metal mold or metal mixing bowl. With back of spoon, smooth ice cream so it is equally distributed over bottom and sides of mold, leaving the center hollow. Freeze until firm, at least 2 hours. Soften the Spumoni ice cream and spoon into the hollowed center, packing it down. Freezer wrap; freeze. To unmold, place mold ice-cream side down on a chilled serving plate. Dip a cloth into hot water, wring out, and press around the mold until the ice cream mold loosens, repeat if necessary. Return to freezer until about 5 minutes before serving. Pass Holly Berry Sauce, if desired.

*Or Pralines 'n Cream Ice Cream and Eggnog Ice Cream.

Holly Berry Sauce

1 package (10 ounces)
   frozen raspberries
1 package (10 ounces)
   frozen strawberries

2 tablespoons Triple Sec or
   frozen orange juice
   concentrate

Defrost frozen berries slightly; pour off juice. Put berries and Triple Sec in blender container. Whirl just until smooth; put through sieve. Refrigerate. Makes 10 to 12 servings.

CHRISTMAS SUNDAE PIE

Gingersnap Crust: Mix 1⅓ cups gingersnap crumbs with 6 tablespoons soft butter until crumbly. Press to bottom and sides of a 9-inch pie plate. Bake in a 375-degree oven for 8 minutes. Cool. Freeze.

Filling: Fill frozen crust with one quart of Egg Nog Ice Cream, mounding center. Top with pint of Rum Raisin Ice Cream, swirling top. Top with grated, unsweetened chocolate or chopped walnuts.

ENGLISH TOFFEE SUNDAE SQUARES

1 cup sifted flour
¼ cup crunchy Granola
¼ cup packed brown sugar
½ cup butter
½ cup chopped walnuts
1 jar (9¾ ounces) Baskin-Robbins Butterscotch Topping

1 quart Baskin-Robbins English Toffee Ice Cream
Whipped cream or topping, optional
Maraschino cherries, optional

In bowl, combine flour, Granola, and brown sugar. Cut butter into mixture until it looks like coarse crumbs; stir in nuts. Pat mixture into a 9″ × 13″ × 2″ baking pan. Bake for 15 minutes in a preheated 400-degree oven. While still warm, stir to crumble mixture. Cool. Spread *half* of crumb mixture in a 9″ × 9″ × 2″ pan. Drizzle half of the butterscotch topping over crumbs. Slightly soften ice cream; carefully spread over crumbs. Drizzle with remaining topping; sprinkle with remaining crumbs. Freeze at least 2 hours. To serve: remove from freezer about 5 minutes before cutting into squares or bars. If desired, top each serving with whipped cream and a cherry. Makes 9 to 12 servings.

Frances Raab, Chelmsford, Massachusetts (1973)

PEPPERMINT NOG PUNCH

1 quart Egg Nog Ice
    Cream
1 quart Peppermint Ice
    Cream
1 bottle (28 ounces)
    chilled club soda

Few drops of red food
    coloring
½ cup whipping cream,
    whipped

Blend first 4 ingredients in punchbowl. Top with whipped cream. Makes 18 to 20 punch cups.

EASY CHERRIES JUBILEE

Heat ¼ cup currant jelly and one drained can of bing cherries (1 pound, 4 ounces) just to boiling, stirring. Serve warm over Fresh Strawberry or Fresh Coconut Ice Cream. In a small saucepan, slightly heat 3 tablespoons brandy over low heat. Pour over cherry mixture; light with match. Serve flaming over ice cream.

New Year's Eve

That pretty much does it. Our year-long ice cream world is about ready to come to a close. If you haven't come up with a nice long list of ice cream favorites by this time, then you just don't rate as a bona fide ice cream freak (certainly not a Baskin-Robbins freak!) and we suggest you look around and find something else to be your favorite food.

New Year's Eve is a special time when people tend to go wild, throwing fate to the wind and forgetting that tomorrow is, indeed, just as near around the corner as it is any other day. Not to throw a wet blanket on the celebrations, but it would be our sober advice to exercise a little caution (if not restraint) and perhaps reflect a bit on the passing of the year. Look back at what was accomplished during the year that's ending, and look ahead at the challenges of the one to come.

We hope this book has helped to brighten a day or two in your life already, and that it will continue to do so as you keep on reading and trying the many different types of recipes you've found here. Maybe you've found a favorite or two in the course of reading the book; why not pick out your favorite and

serve it again on New Year's Eve, perhaps re-creating the mood of the occasion during the past year when you originally served it?

At age 31, Baskin-Robbins has only just come of age. Thirty-one is certainly considered the prime of life. There are as many flavor—and recipe—possibilities as there are ice cream fans in the world. Baskin-Robbins plans to keep right on "Making People Happy"—for another one hundred and thirty-one years! There's no time limit to magic!

CHECK WHICH TITLES HAVE THE MOST APPEAL FOR YOU!

Pinnacle Books proudly presents a list of
books that can bring you new health
and increased happiness.

Check which books you'd like to own:

_____ZONE THERAPY: A Guide to Applied-Pressure Therapy by Anika Bergson & Vladimir Tuchack   P456 $1.25

_____FOOD TO IMPROVE YOUR HEALTH: A Complete Guide to Over 300 Foods for 101 Common Ailments by Linda Pelstring & Jo Ann Hauck   P637 $1.50

_____HOW TO HELP YOUR DOCTOR HELP YOU by Jessyca Russell Gaver   P587 $1.75

_____RELAXERCISES: Remodel Yourself the Rhythmic Way by Joan Fraser. Fully illustrated   P088 $1.25

_____BODYMIND: The Whole Person Health Book by Don Ethan Miller   P566 $1.50

_____PSYCHOSOMATICS: How Your Emotions Can Damage Your Health by Howard R. and Martha E. Lewis   P532 $1.75

and a top bestseller:

_____THE THIN BOOK, By a Formerly Fat Psychiatrist, Theodore Isaac Rubin, M.D.
    P777 $1.25

Check which books you want. If you can't find any of these books at your local bookstore, simply send cover price plus 25¢ per book for postage and handling to:
PINNACLE BOOKS,
275 Madison Avenue, New York, N.Y. 10016

The
Thin Book

By A Formerly Fat Psychiatrist

Theodore Isaac Rubin, M.D.

**The famous bestselling guide
to healthful weight control:
medically authoritative,
scientifically accurate,
psychologically sound.**

The fascinating story behind
the greatest naval adventures of all time:
the saga of Horatio Hornblower

The

Hornblower
Companion

C.S. FORESTER

The complete and indispensable guide.
Fully illustrated with maps, charts, and drawings
by Samuel H. Bryant

P440   THE HORNBLOWER COMPANION $1.95

TO ORDER

Please check the space next to the book/s you want, send this order
form together with your check or money order, include the price of
the book/s and 25¢ for handling and mailing to:

PINNACLE BOOKS, INC. / P.O. Box 4347
Grand Central Station / New York, N.Y. 10017

☐ CHECK HERE IF YOU WANT A FREE CATALOG

I have enclosed $_____check_____or money order_____
as payment in full. No C.O.D.'s

Name_____

Address_____

City_____State_____Zip_____
(Please allow time for delivery)